The History of
BREAD

The History of
BREAD

BERNARD DUPAIGNE

Translated from the French by Antonio and Sylvie Roder

HARRY N. ABRAMS, INC., PUBLISHERS

For the English-Language Edition

PROJECT MANAGER: Ellen Nidy

EDITOR: Adele Westbrook

DESIGN COORDINATOR: Barbara Sturman

Recipes compiled and edited by Camille Le Foll

Graphic Design by Rampazzo and Associates

Library of Congress Cataloging-in-Publication Data

Dupaigne, Bernard.

    The history of bread / by Bernard Dupaigne.

       p.   cm.

    ISBN 0–8109–3438–8

    1. Bread—History.   I. Title.

TX769.D83   1999

641.8'15'09—dc21   99–22309

Printed and bound in Italy

Harry N. Abrams, Inc.

100 Fifth Avenue

New York, N.Y. 10011

www.abramsbooks.com

Foreword

Bread is the symbol of shared food, the very essence of life. It is the fruit of protracted toil and is deeply anchored in our civilization. Whether made of wheat, barley, or rye, bread illuminates our history and our evolution, as does rice in Asia, millet or manioc in Africa, and yams or taro in Oceania.

Bread is an object of unparalleled worship and decorum. It embodies the full cycle of life and seasons, from the death of the wheat kernel in the earth to its resurrection as a stalk, from its ordeal in the mill to its journey through the oven and its offering at the table. Bread is a part of all major events in many lives, from birth, to betrothal and marriage, to death and resurrection.

Bread is integral to life. It is the source of many childhood emotions recaptured: the tempting smell wafting from the bakery oven, the pleasure of lingering there, breathing in the warm and nourishing aroma of baking bread.

Bernard Dupaigne

Contents

THE HISTORY OF BREAD

As a major event in mankind's history, the birth of bread can be traced back to the time when people began to crush grains, grind them, and mix them with water, rather than just boil them. In Babylon and ancient Egypt, raised, oven-baked bread coexisted with unleavened flatbread. Then, thanks to the influence of Greece and Rome, people all around the Mediterranean basin started to make bread. Polytheistic civilizations offered white bread to their gods, while Christianity considered consecrated bread to be the body of Christ. In the Middle Ages, monks cut down woods to clear land for new wheat fields. White bread became the staple of lordly tables, while tenant farmers and farmhands had to reconcile themselves to eating black bread. With agricultural mechanization, the nineteenth century saw an improvement in the quality of bread, as prices were reduced and white bread became a commodity within almost everyone's reach. Nevertheless, famine, or at least hunger, continues to haunt the world, thus confirming that the history of bread is inextricably linked to the history of humankind.

Left: **In the Neolithic era, wild or already cultivated grains were crushed and ground on a flat stone to make gruels or flat cakes.**

Opposite: **Grinding grain in the Neolithic era. Rock painting, Tassili des Ajjers.**

Above: **Kneading bread dough in a stone trough in Palestine (ninth to seventh century B.C.).**

Opposite: **Encampment. Ashurbanipal Palace bas-relief, Assyria, seventh century** B.C.

disposal, but it is also possible to make a porridge by plunging heated stones into a mixture of starches and water contained in a wooden vessel, or even by placing the mixture into a hole in the ground. This was the method used by the indigenous inhabitants of California to prepare the acorns of various oaks that comprised their diet, and to eliminate their bitterness. Boiling with heated stones was known in Europe and is still used today in Oceania to make porridges from nourishing tubers.

"The Bread You Drink"

In Central Europe, the use of heated stones was widespread in the ancient art of brewing—the making of beer having been a popular way of using starches, particularly cereals, since antiquity, in both the Old and New World. We can even speculate that, for a time, some people may have been nourished primarily by some sort of beer which, after all, is actually a kind of fermented gruel, a "bread you drink"—this is apparent in the case of the Slavic *kvass* or the fermented millet porridge known as *bràgà*.

One great achievement was to domesticate fermentation by the controlled preparation of yeast, first in Babylon, then in ancient Egypt. "In Babylon, nearly three thousand years before our era, the fermentation of boiled grains to produce beer had already been mastered and, in all likelihood, domesticated yeast was also used to make fermented flat cakes that were already tantamount to bread." Clay tablets from Babylon (seventeenth century B.C.) refer to bread-making. This control of fermentation, together with the selection of cereals high in gluten content and, therefore, increasingly suitable for bread-making, paved the way for unleavened flatbread or leavened loaves as a primary mode of cereal consumption.

The history of bread begins less than ten thousand years ago in Asia Minor, with the domestication of wild grain in the mountains and foothills of the Fertile Crescent. That is where a "Neolithic revolution" took place, with a transition from the adaptation of natural elements to the production of cultivated resources—a springboard for our societies and civilizations.

It is probable that one of the most ancient ways of cooking the grains of wild grasses was grilling. Until recent times, that is how gatherers in the regions of India, Malaysia, and Oceania prepared *Coïx lacryma-jobi* grains, or Job's tears, a grass whose seed is used from India to China and New Guinea. However, it is also likely that boiling whole, cracked, or finely ground grain represents a very ancient practice. This method is certainly easier when the cook has clay pots at his or her

BREAD OF THE PHARAOHS

The Egyptians were very knowledgeable about the fermentation of dough and the use of ovens (which made it possible to bake thick loaves that had risen through fermentation). There is evidence of this in a number of their tomb frescoes that illustrate bakeries with well-structured working methods. Kneading is done by foot or by hand, in which case two men squat face-to-face with the dough between them. Flatbreads are baked on a slab set over a wood fire, while thicker breads go into the oven. The oven is cylindrical, open at the top, or shaped like those still found in Asia and in certain Mediterranean countries: a cone truncated at the top, within which the flat cakes are slapped against the inner walls. Herodotus, in the fifth century B.C., mentions Egyptian bread leavened and baked in a brick oven which the Hebrews called *tannurim*. The same kind of oven is still called a *tanûr* in Iran and Yemen.

The Pharaohs maintained production in their palace bakeries on a truly impressive scale. During the thirty years of his reign, Ramses III distributed some six million sacks of wheat and seven million loaves of bread to the temples. Bread was used in those days as payment in kind. The daily wage for agricultural laborers was three loaves of bread and two pitchers of beer. Functionaries were paid with leavened bread, or with the less desirable, unleavened flatbread. The annual remuneration for a temple functionary amounted to 360 pitchers of beer and 900 bread loaves of first quality wheat, as well as 36,000 pancakes baked in ashes—and yet, he would still complain about the pitiful number of leavened loaves.

In Egypt there were at least fifteen varieties of bread: flat cakes with a circular design in the center and around the sides, or pierced with eight holes in a circle, or a triangular shape, or folded in half, and wheat or mixed-grain breads; breads shaped like disks, mounds, cones, spirals, or crescents; honey bread, yeast bread, bread leavened with the same brewer's yeast that was used for the beer offered to priests or at court. Other breads, made of dough fried in oil, were fashioned in animal or even human form.

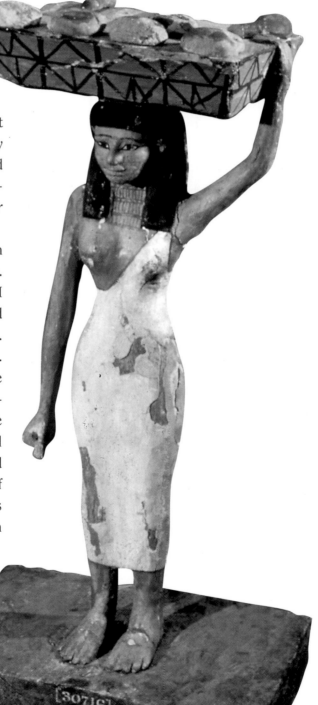

BREAD OF ANCIENT GREECE

Originally, the diet of Greek shepherds consisted of cereal porridges and flat cakes. Greek vases dating from the sixth century B.C. show cakes baked over a wood fire, then rolled up for conservation. Later, the reforms introduced by Solon (639–559 B.C.) in Athens to break up large estates and redistribute land for the benefit of small holdings, encouraged the cultivation of barley. By 500 B.C., the consumption of barley bread and flat cakes became widespread.

However, since the production of barley in Greece was never sufficient, the massive importation of wheat from Sicily, Egypt, the remote shores of the Black Sea, and Southern Russia was necessary to give full scope to the Greek baking tradition and the development of a veritable art of breadmaking. In fact, conquests were often the result of expeditions undertaken to search for new sources and supplies of wheat. In Athens, one million *médimnes* of wheat, or one-third of the cereal consumption, was imported.

The Greek historian Athenaeus (third century A.D.), writing about the Classical Era, mentions no less than seventy-two varieties of bread served at the most ordinary as well as the most lavish meals: barley bread *(cyphes)* for the poor and for slaves; rye bread imported from Egypt *(olyra)*; *chondrites* made from spelt or bearded wheat flour,

which Typhon of Alexandria classified as unfermented along with the *syncomiste* made of wheat; *octablomoi,* round loaves marked into eighths by four lines crossing at the center, and made of more or less well sifted wheat flour; *lecythite* prepared with oil, or *destreptitie* made with milk, oil, and pepper; the cheese bread *tyronte;* or else the twice-baked *dipyre.* Sometimes, the bread was flavored with herbs—sesame, poppy, or anise seed. Honey bread *(melitate* or *escharite)* was also quite widespread in the countryside and is mentioned by several Athenian philosophers and politicians such as Pythagoras (580–500 B.C.), Themistocles (525–460 B.C.), Socrates (470–399 B.C.), and Demosthenes (384–322 B.C.).

But white bread, such as *amilois,* prepared from well sifted wheat flour, was already preferred above all the others. Aristophanes (445–386 B.C.), highly praised its whiteness and the quality of its flavor. The bakeries of Athens and Megara had the best reputations.

The Greeks did not merely obtain yeast from leftover dough, as had been the practice in Egypt, instead, they learned to produce it at grape harvest time from a mixture of hops and grape must. Some yeasts were kept in cool storage for several months in small amphoras.

Opposite: **Great Eleusinian celebrations at the Temple of Demeter, Eleusis, Greece. Demeter, with her daughter Persephone, presents the first wheat stalk, bearing the knowledge of agriculture, to Triptoleme, King of Eleusis. Votive relief, fifth century B.C.**

Below: **Women of Greek antiquity kneading dough in a workshop to the sound of a flute.**

18

The Cult of Demeter

Demeter is the Greek goddess of agriculture. She is the Goddess-Mother figure of classical antiquity, mother of humanity and of the nurturing earth, who brings and furthers fertility; she is the "mistress of the great loaves." Her daughter Persephone, abducted by Hades, god of the underworld, has fallen under the spell of the magical pomegranate and must forever spend one-third of the year in dusky shadow, and the other two-thirds near her mother in the company of the other gods.

The myth of Persephone's death and resurrection celebrates the labor associated with sowing the grains of wheat. It is akin to the legend of Joseph, son of Jacob, thrown into a well by his brothers but reborn all-powerful in Egypt, where he distributes bread to his starving people; or to the story of Isis, the Egyptian goddess of fertility who reassembles the body of her spouse, Osiris, which had been cut into fourteen pieces and thrown into the Nile, thus resurrecting him as the bearer of abundance.

In Greece, every year around September 20, the Great Eleusinian celebrations were held at the sanctuary of Demeter in Eleusis, marking the beginning of Persephone's four-month sojourn under the earth. The initiates would then descend to the subterranean world so that they might be reborn in the vibrant harvest light. Little or nothing is known to this day about these mysterious ceremonies, whose secrets were jealously guarded by the participants.

The first grains were dedicated to Demeter. During the agrarian feast of Thargélies, the first loaves made from the new wheat were eaten in a special ritual. This offering ceremony took place during the harvest month, the eleventh month of the Athenian year (mid-May to mid-June), aptly named *thargélion* after the first loaves or cakes, the *thargelos,* made from the newly harvested flour.

"It was before sleep comes. Our eyes were closed. We were stretched out rigid as the dead under icy sheets. We were letting our own warmth gradually suffuse us. I was thinking about the Eleusinian Demeter so beloved of all Mediterranean mountain people. The path which descends to the center of the earth where she lays. Not at all like those white stone steps which wander through all the Odyssean villages down to the sea, but rather a gentle earthen slope plunging deeper and deeper into darkness. Not, I thought, a market stairway running from village to ship to sell jars, to buy lotus blossoms from sailors with goat-like eyes. Not at all. Rather, a friendly incline . . . because we are descending to the blossoming fields of the underworld. We are already stroked by the yellow scent of asphodels as it reaches up to us. And it is not the weight of the baskets of bread they bear on their heads that slows the women's gait, that ennobles the sway of their hospitable loins, but the growing nearness of regions of peace and of joy.

Oh Demeter, heavy with Adonis and the wild boar as well, nurturer of life, you who rejoice in scythes and the scattering of seed, give us sweet concord, true treasures, and health.

Then, we fell asleep. Everyone must have been sleeping, because the silence and the frost had suddenly gained a terrifying freedom."

(Jean Giono, *Les Vraies Richesses*)

Opposite: **Persephone, held captive in the underworld by Hades, offers a sheaf of wheat and a rooster. Votive plaque, late sixth century or early fifth century** B.C.

ROME OR ARS PISTORICA

Was bread a staple in Rome in the fourth century B.C.? A legend relates how the Romans, under siege and close to capitulating to the Gauls in 390 B.C., found deliverance—with some divine assistance. It seems that their general, Camillus, was admonished by Jupiter in a dream to convert what little flour they had left into loaves of bread and to hurl them at their besiegers. This maneuver was intended to convince their attackers that abundance reigned and that they were still a long way from seizing a stronghold which they had thought they could starve into surrender. While this anecdote related by the historians of antiquity remains unconfirmed, it nevertheless highlights the major role bread played in Roman civilization.

Like the Greeks, the Romans subsisted for a long time on porridges made of cereals, on grilled barley, or on flatbread. This form of nourishment became so common among them that other nations even nicknamed them the *Pultiphagi Romani* or "porridge eaters." By contrast, the main food-related activities among Celts and Germanic people were fishing, hunting, and animal husbandry as a source of meat.

According to Pliny, it was only in 168 B.C., when the armies of Perseus I, king of Macedonia, were annihilated by the Roman Legions, that the art of breadmaking truly began to develop in Rome, stimulated by the Greek bakers taken into slavery. Bakery scenes sculpted on sarcophagi or bas-reliefs (100 B.C.) testify to this *ars pistorica*. The importance of bakeries in Rome increased to the point that, at the threshold of the Christian Era, under the reign of Augustus, the first emperor, they numbered 329 for a population of slightly more than one million. Bread was even carried in religious ceremonial processions. For example, on June 8, festival day for both vestal virgins and bakers, donkeys adorned with flower crowns and bread roll necklaces were paraded through the streets of Rome.

The most typical Roman bread was a flattened half-round loaf, divided in four by two crossed lines, the *quadra panis*. The breads were named

Below: **Portrayal of the Last Supper, early Christian era. Sarcophagus, third century A.D.**

according to their grains and the quality of the milling. Coarse and mixed-grain breads were for the general populace, while for the nobility, there was bread baked from the finest wheat, very white and flavorful. Slaves, peasants, city dwellers, senators, all bought the bread appropriate to their social status: *sordidus,* whole-meal and bran bread; the unleavened and heavy *athletarum;* and various rustic breads, *panis plebeius,* made with crudely sifted flour containing milling waste; and *panis secondaris,* prepared with second-quality flour.

The finest of fine flours was reserved for the choicest white luxury breads: the *panis palatius* intended for the Imperial household. Sophocles wrote: "You will be celebrated, beloved Italy, for your white grain."

In Rome, bread was generally leavened with dough from the previous day; but due perhaps to Gallic influence, the use of brewer's yeast gained in popularity. Pliny the Elder (A.D. 23–79) describes the yeast production process in his *Natural History:* "In Spain and Gaul, they make a drink whose thick foam serves to leaven bread. This is why bread is lighter in those parts than anywhere else." For banquets and special occasions, bakers would create a whole series of decorated breads to order: intertwined hearts for weddings, lyre-shaped bread in honor of poets, small rolls with spiral spokes, called *panis candidus,* and others in the shape of keys, dice, or braids. There was even a special bread called *ostrearius,* served with oysters, which were consumed in large quantities. *Furfurens* was a bread sprinkled with anise or poppy seed; other breads were enriched with milk, oil, and eggs, or else baked in oiled terra-cotta molds, or on a spit. Even dietetic breads were already available, such as *pepsianus, spensiticus,* and *dygesticus.* Writers celebrated the highly prized "Persian bread," whose

Above: **Ceres, goddess of the earth and harvests. Mosaic, third century** A.D.

Pages 24–25: **Baking leavened bread in a horizontal floor oven very similar to contemporary European ovens. Gallo-Roman mosaic.**

dough contained a lot of water, which is why it was also called *panis aquaticus*. The popularity of this Asian bread, quite different from Roman bread, demonstrates that the ancient East had not depended upon Egypt for the discovery of bread.

Pompeii had over forty well-organized bakery shops, in addition to the domestic ovens in every home. In one of these commercial bakeries there was a large brick oven, quite similar to the old-fashioned ovens in many European countrysides, with a flat hearth and a vaulted roof. Nearby in the same room were the flour mills, up to four in a row, which suggests the scale of bread production. These mills were an improvement on the conical stone system invented in Italy circa 250 B.C.—the stationary stone or "sleeper," set on the ground, was cut into a conical shape. On top of it sat the fitted, movable, hollow stone whose top flared out to accept the grain. The space between the two stones gradually narrowed so that the kernels would be crushed increasingly fine as they traveled down inside the mill, running out at the bottom as fine flour. The grindstone was probably turned by slaves, two to each mill.

Opposite: **Roman bakery. Mural painting, Pompeii, first century** B.C.

Below: **Multiplication of the loaves: the barley loaves and the two fishes. Mosaic, fifth century** A.D.

Bread and Circuses

he Romans had a maxim that with bread and circuses, they could lead the people wherever they pleased. In order to prevent unrest, Rome even started to distribute wheat to its neediest citizens, freeborn or freed, noble or common, who numbered 200,000 when Julius Caesar was crowned in 48 B.C. Each of these recipients was given a token, the *tessera frumentaria,* minted first in bronze and later in lead stamped with the effigy of successive emperors. Augustus extended the range of this aid to include agricultural workers who had fallen on hard times, and Nero added the Praetorian cohorts and military guardsmen to the ranks of those entitled to such assistance.

Under Aurelian, and then Marcus Aurelius bread was distributed instead of wheat, each beneficiary receiving two loaves a day, with about 300,000 recipients by that time. This bread was called *panis civilis,* to differentiate it from *panis gradilis,* which was handed out to circus audiences before the games.

Despite the precautions and the vigilance of magistrates and officers, these gestures of generosity provoked the same excesses and the same insurrections under the emperors as they had under the Republic, thus contributing to the downfall of Rome. An aristocracy enriched by colonial trade and a mass of landless, idle peasants were a danger to authority and quick to embrace the party of any tribune who made eloquent promises. According to the famous formula in Juvenal's *Satires,* the only demand this unemployed population could formulate was for *panem et circences,* "bread and circuses." Consequently, when the Barbarians arrived, Rome and its civilization were ripe for collapse and foundered in A.D. 476.

Left: **Joseph Marie Vien,** *Marcus Aurelius Ordering the Distribution of Medicaments,* **1765. Amiens, Musée de Picardie.**

BREAD IN THE BIBLE

The Hebrews of early Biblical times were nomadic shepherds subsisting on the meat of their sheep. As Genesis tells us, God had regard only for Abel, the shepherd, and for his offering, scorning Cain, the farmer, and his gift. Obeying the dictates of migratory herding, the sons of Israel wandered as far as Egypt, where they settled down and turned to animal husbandry. And it was probably through contact with the Egyptians that the Hebrews acquired a taste for bread, which they had previously known only as unleavened flat cakes cooked on hot stones.

Leaving Egypt under the Pharaohs of the Nineteenth Dynasty, the Jews took their flocks with them. But according to Scripture, bread is what they missed the most *(Exodus, XVI, 3);* they bitterly complained about this, even after receiving manna, "the bread of heaven." At last, upon reaching the land of Canaan, they became farmers who improved the land. From that time onward, God began to love the sedentary people and agrarian parables multiply in the Old Testament: "If ye follow my laws, and keep my commandments, and put them into practice, then I will give you rain in due season. And your threshing shall reach unto the vintage, and the vintage shall reach unto the sowing time: and ye shall eat your bread to the full" *(Leviticus, XXVI, 3).*

Bread was henceforth the offering made to God at the altar of the Tabernacle, in the Temple of Yahweh. In those days, the twelve "showbreads" were merely presented and offered to God, then removed and replaced with warm loaves *(Samuel, XXI, 6).* God loves the smell of wheat and the offerings of bread.

Those who were wealthy ate leavened bread made of fine wheat flour; the bread of those less fortunate was composed of barley flour *(Ruth, II, 23)* which cost half the price of the other *(Kings, VII, 1).* Unleavened cakes were left to the shepherds, who were still nomads. As in ancient Greece, women were the bread-makers: they ground the flour on a stone handmill *(Exodus, XI, 5),* and they baked the bread in the family oven *(Samuel, VIII, 13).*

The advent of Christianity, some thirteen centuries after the Exodus, would confer upon bread an even more considerable religious aura. Through Jesus, bread would become God incarnate: bread alone was viewed with enough respect to embody the Christ figure.

Jesus multiplied barley loaves to feed those assembled to hear his teachings. "And when he had taken the five loaves and the two fishes, he looked up to heaven, and blessed, and broke the loaves, and gave [them] to his disciples to set before them. And they did all eat, and were filled; and they took up twelve baskets full of the fragments of bread that remained" *(Mark, VI, 41 to 43)*. The day after the multiplication of the loaves, in the Capernaum synagogue, Jesus, addressing the crowd, compared himself to bread and identified with it: ". . . my Father giveth you the true bread from heaven; for the bread of God is he which cometh down from heaven, and giveth life unto the world [. . .] I am the bread of life. He that cometh to me shall never hunger [. . .] For my flesh is nourishment indeed." A hard notion, and many of his disciples complained: "This is a hard saying; who can hear it?" *(John, VI, 32 to 60)*.

The Last Supper marked the final step in this identification with bread. On that day, while performing the sacrifice of the Jewish Passover, Jesus took some bread—unleavened—and declared to his twelve disciples that this bread had become his own body. This last meal during which Christ, surrounded by his apostles, instituted the Eucharist, was to become a favorite theme in Renaissance painting.

The liturgy of the Mass is inspired by Jewish traditions consisting of blessings, acts of grace, and the ritual of a shared meal. The Catholic religion then follows age-old Mediterranean traditions by sanctifying bread, wine, and oil. Anglo-Saxon Protestantism, on the other hand, is more oriented toward meat and pork products. Europe thus reconciles the Roman cult of bread with the Celtic taste for meat.

Left: **El Greco, *The Last Supper*, c. 1565.**
Jesus and his twelve disciples share
bread for the last time.

The Communion Wafer

Until the year 1000, Catholics partaking of Communion used bread decorated with motifs that were impressed using terra-cotta seals. But the Pope, realizing that Christ could only have eaten unleavened bread at Easter time, transformed the eucharistic bread into an unleavened Communion wafer, which, since the time of Saint Thomas Aquinas in 1250, has been made from very pure, very fine, very white wheat flour.

Communion wafers *(altar bread, singing bread)* could be made by the faithful. In France, they were also made by special bakers called "Pâtissiers-Oublieurs" (from *oublieur,* another name for the wafer). But they have long been made principally in convents. The dough is shaped while hot using a special iron, a long handled and often very beautiful mold.

The wafers are generally circular, evoking infinity, perfection, the eternity of God. The small ones intended for the faithful are plain, while those meant for the priest are three times larger and stamped with religious motifs. The Benedictines at 66-bis avenue Denfert-Rochereau in Paris still make 200,000 Communion wafers a month, and those of Pernes-les-Fontaine, in the Vaucluse region, produce 22 million of them a year!

Down through the ages, ignorance and superstition have lent an almost magical value to the consecrated Host, a true object of desire on the part of those who would appropriate its power for their own ends. Because of his presence in the bread, God could become a pawn of hatred. Tabernacles were locked shut; stolen wafers were profaned, defiled, scorned. But it was said that the Host will bleed when a heathen, indulging in a sacrilegious act of madness, stabs it with a knife; or that the wafer can denounce a thief, or make itself so heavy that the robber cannot pry it from the tabernacle. Other miraculous Hosts were said to be indestructible. It was related that, in Holland, a wafer was given to an invalid who could not swallow it; thrown into the fire, it did not burn. And this miracle gave rise to a great devotional pilgrimage. Black masses duplicated the sacrament of the Eucharist in reverse. The "officiating clergyman" ate a Communion wafer on the bare belly of a woman. In such an atmosphere of exacerbated superstitious fanaticism, thousands of people were burned alive after being accused of making the Host bleed; the bleeding Host is one of the most astonishing collective delusions on record and has led to appalling deeds. The Jews were the first to be accused of this sacrilege: in 1253, the entire Jewish community was burned in the little town of Beelitz, near Berlin; in 1290, a similar event occurred in Paris, and eight years later, in Kornneuburg, near Vienna. Stakes were lit throughout central Europe.[1] On May 22, 1370, several hundred Jews were burned in Paris because Hosts had allegedly bled in the Sainte-Gudule church; and again, thirty-eight Berlin Jews were burned in 1510. On October 26, 1848, before the Berlin Academy of Science, the German naturalist Gottfried Ehrenberg (1795–1876) proved

Left: **Bartolomeo,** *Saint Barbe*
with Goblet and Host, 1497.

that the phenomenon of the so-called bleeding Host was due simply to a bacteria later named *Bacillus prodigiosus.*

Orthodox practitioners use leavened, everyday bread that has been consecrated by the use of a seal. This is still done in certain Catholic monasteries where the consecrated bread is the same as the bread eaten at meals. There have also been modern innovations at some churches where pieces of consecrated bread are passed along to the congregation in a basket during Communion—those who wish to take Communion help themselves. Others use a specially created and decorated eucharistic bread. In Syriac rites, a circle of dough is imprinted with a seal that produces twelve sections, each of which is marked with a dot: the priest breaks the bread, keeps the central portion, and distributes the rest to the faithful. In Greece and Bulgaria, the bread used during the Mass is round, made of finely sifted white flour, and stamped with a wooden seal that imprints designs evoking Christ and the implements of the Passion: a stylized tomb, the lance and sponge of the Crucifixion surrounding the Virgin, sometimes the pincers, the hammer, and the whip of flagellation. The center bears a three-level, thrice-repeated inscription in Greek or Cyrillic characters transcribed as *IS XS NI KA,* meaning "Jesus-Christ Victorious" *(Iesous XristoS Nika* in Greek, and in Cyrillic, *Isus XristoS Nika).* Alternately, the first two letters of *Xristos* may be used instead of the first and last: *IsuS Xristos Nika.*

Some of these breads bear the crowned two-headed eagle, emblem of the Orthodox Church. During the service, the priest cuts a central square from this bread, which he will dip in wine, while he distributes the other pieces among the faithful during Communion. These eucharistic breads are brought to Mass by the faithful, who nowadays order them from the baker. They are offered as ex-votos to celebrate a birthday or anniversary. Any unconsecrated bread that has not been used for the Eucharist is blessed and given to charity.

The Last Supper

Christ multiplied, endlessly returning in the eucharistic bread: what a bold concept! It is a democratic God, perceptible to all, present in the world and present within each believer through communion. It is a God of love, different from the gods of fear who are unfathomable and inaccessible. Unhallowed at the beginning of the mass, the bread of the Eucharist becomes God at the moment of consecration: "Take and eat, for this is my body, this is my blood!"

Must we hold that Christ actually descends into the wafer during consecration, and that this wafer has become the body of Christ for the faithful to eat? Or is the consecration simply a symbolic gesture intended as a reminder that Christ broke bread with his disciples as a sign of communion, to symbolize the unity of the faithful?

Christians have long remained divided on this issue. But in 1215, the Fourth Lateran Council, under Pope Innocent III, proclaimed that during consecration Christ really did enter the bread. Christ *is* the bread, and Roman Catholics actually consume His flesh and blood. This doctrine of transubstantiation was one of the factors which caused the Protestants to separate from the Church of Rome.

Opposite: **Jaime Ferrer,** *The Last Supper,*
**detail, fifteenth century. Spain, Solsona,
Diocesan Museum.**

BREAD SINCE THE MIDDLE AGES

In the Western world, the forests were cleared by monks living among Gauls and Germanic people who were still uninterested in agriculture. The abbeys had their own—sometimes sizable—bakeries: the oven at the abbey of Saint-Gall is said to have had a capacity of several hundred loaves. Beginning in the twelfth century, with the coalescence of feudal power, peasants were compelled to bring their wheat to the mill owned by their lord, and to bake their dough in the collective or "common" oven, for which the lord also collected additional taxes. The peasants ate poorly sifted, inferior bread full of bran. This bread was eaten mainly in the form of a *soupe,* denoting a slice of bread at the bottom of a bowlful of broth. Gargantua's expressions, *tailler des soupes* (to slice bread) or *tremper la soupe* (to pour broth over bread slices), are no longer heard but were part of the daily language in those days. A meal at the castle or at the table of a wealthy bourgeois, on the other hand, was a different story: cuts of meat were served on large slices of country bread called *tranchoirs* (slicers), "half a foot wide and four fingers thick." According to the *Mesnagier de Paris,* a famous collection of household tips written circa 1393, "these bread slices—soaked with gravy and fat—were never eaten by the guests, but were collected later in an alms basket, tray, or pot and distributed to the servants or to the poor who had been waiting at the door until the gentry finished their meal." Royal coronations, in particular, were occasions for preparing these slices of bread in great numbers—some 1,294 dozen of them were served at the coronation of Louis XII in 1498, and the same ritual was still being performed when Charles IX was crowned in 1560. The custom of eating meat on these *tranchoirs* persisted in Europe until the seventeenth century, notably in Poland. Beginning in the fourteenth century, however, *pains blancs de bouche,* fine white bread, began to make an appearance at certain tables. Until then, bread had been more or less white, mixed or not with barley and rye, depending upon social standing. Old charters cited by Du Cange in his *Glos-*

saire de la basse latinité (Glossary of Low Latin Usage) bear witness to the diversity of bread: court bread, knight's bread, groom or servant bread, canon's bread or dining-hall bread, as well as the bread of the people, ball-shaped loaves of rye, barley, and wheat.

Bread Laws

In the Middle Ages, bread was the most common, most essential, and most indispensable of all foods. No one would think of doing without; it was part of all meals, served with all dishes, and often the only food available to the poor. The extreme importance of this staple in feudal society is evidenced by the countless ordinances, edicts, and regulations passed during the reigns of successive kings concerning its production and sale, the codes that had to be observed by bakers, and the severity of sanctions that were to be imposed on violators. As the Roman government had understood, bread was a basic factor in maintaining social stability and peace; it therefore continued to receive the full attention of sovereign rulers, and it assumed a distinctive symbolic value in Christendom.

Thus, in the eighth century, Charlemagne controlled the price of grains, prohibiting their export in order to limit speculation, and establish-

Below: **Rudolf von Ems, drawing of a horizontal oven. From *La Chronique du Monde (Chronicle of the World),* fourteenth century.**

Above: **A baker and his wife standing in front of their shop in a Flanders town. The horizontal oven juts out over the street. Miniature from the *Decameron*, Boccacio, 1432.**

ing selling prices: one *denier* per bushel for oats, two *deniers* for barley, and four for wheat—a price scale that provides an interesting indication of the value attributed to each type of cereal at the time. He even ordered that the grains produced on his own lands be sold below the rates that he had set.

In the cities, the bakers—who had been organized into guilds since the twelfth century—had to comply with very specific ordinances regarding the quality, the weight, and the price of bread. "In 1372, under Charles V, they had the right to make three kinds of bread corresponding to various grades of sifted flour"—white burgher's bread, brown bread, and black rye bread—"endowed with all its finest flour and bran."[2] Militia officers made regular inspections, and neither "lame bread," as defective loaves were called, nor "ratted bread" nibbled by rats and mice, could be sold—such bread was usually given away to the poor.

In England, Jean sans Terre (John Lackland,

1167–1216) set the price of bread according to the price of wheat; and in 1266, the *Assisa panis* of his son and successor, Henry III, limited the baker's net profit to 13%. The etymology of the word for bread, *loaf,* is revealing, coming as it does from the root *half,* which has given us both *loaf* and *lord*—the lord dispenses the bread. In the City of London, laws regulating the baker's trade forbade the adulteration of flour through the addition of different grain mixtures. Much later, in the early nineteenth century, a law authorized the sale of such breads—wheat mixed with other flours—but stipulated that the baker must mark them with a large *M,* standing for mixed.

Bread laws also included ad hoc measures to accommodate particular circumstances and disasters. For instance, due to a shortage or the exorbitant cost of bread, the Paris Parliament in September 1740 forbade the baking of any kind of bread but white bran. It also prohibited soft bread and small rolls, and surprisingly, the flour-based powder widely used on wigs at the time.

Market Reports

Despite countless measures and regulations throughout the centuries, bread remained a source of uncertainty, a perennial cause of popular discontent. All too often, bread remained expensive and of poor quality—when not purely and simply unavailable. Despite certain periods of plenty, such as the second half of the fifteenth century, daily bread was synonymous with high costs and shortages.

Early in the sixteenth century, the quality of life worsened, and it continued to deteriorate until the nineteenth century. The figures are staggering. Thanks to reports that list the official tariffs of food products sold on the open market, the exact prices of cereals are known. The oldest available figures are for Paris: from 1500 to 1598, the price of wheat increased tenfold in the capital, while workers' salaries grew only fourfold; in 1450, the daily wage of a Paris laborer was equal to 26 kg of wheat or 43 kg of rye; in 1500, he could no longer afford more than 15 kg of wheat or 25 kg of rye; in 1550, 6 kg of wheat or 10 kg of rye; and in 1600, 5½ kg of wheat or 9 kg of rye.

During the sixteenth century, rural poverty drove unemployed masses from the countryside to Paris, and salaries fell as the available manpower grew. At the same time, it was often difficult to supply the capital due to wars with Spain, Flanders, Germany, and England.

The history of these eras can be summed up as a series of wars, epidemics, and famines, such as those of 1545–1546, 1564, 1572, or the years of the Fronde. Everywhere, the cry was the same: "The people are hungry!"

Vagaries of Climate

There were many contributing factors, beginning with climate changes. Toward the middle of the sixteenth century, the climate of Europe cooled (following a rather warm century from 1340 to 1450) at an average rate of 1°C per year. Harsh winters with persistent frosts were more frequent and the summers were cooler and less sunny, all of which had serious consequences for agriculture and for grain yields. The ability to feed what was essentially still just a peasant society, depended primarily on the luck of the harvest. Certain years were calamitous—after a poor harvest in 1708, the Great Winter of sinister memory caused a general famine. On January 5, 1709, the temperature dropped drastically: at Versailles, the wine froze in Louis XIV's glass and all the rivers soon solidified all the way downstream. Countless vagrants took to the road that winter. The deep cold spell lasted for two months, thus destroying the fall sowing. Prices rose steeply: one *setier* (about 8 liters) of wheat which cost 5 *livres* the previous year increased to 58 *livres*. Whatever measures were taken could only be symbolic—barley bread was served at the king's table and bakers were forbidden to sell white bread.

Substitute Breads

Faced with such chronic shortages, human beings must adapt. Bread was often mixed with second-rate flour: the famine which raged in Naples in 1585 forced the people to eat bread *di castagne e legumi,* made from chestnuts and dried legumes. In sixteenth-century Venice, rice flour was mixed with other flours to produce cheap bread; in the Cévennes region and in Corsica, "tree bread" was made from chestnut flour. In addition, bread was baked less often and almost always eaten hard and moldy. According to Fernand Baudel, "in some regions, one had to cut it with an ax. In the Tyrol, a whole wheat bread made with crushed grain that could be kept a very long time was baked two or three times a year."

Driven by hunger and despair, people adopted flour substitutes, which produced bread in name only. The more destitute turned to drying grape seeds, hazelnuts, and bracken to mix into bread; pine bark was added in Sweden; clay, and especially straw, were often used in those hard times, particularly toward the end of the reign of Louis XIV. In the *Journal* of Dubuisson-Auberay, we read that "while lords ate that beautiful fine wheat bread, golden on the outside and white as snow within,

Opposite: **Polish baker's shop. Miniature from** *La Guilde de Cracovie,* **Balthazar Beham, 1505.**

Das ist der briff und gesetze der becker zu krokaw

W Ir rothmann der Stad Crakow bekenne offentlich
mit disem brieffe das wir mit eintrechtigem rate
der aldten Herrn beschlossen haben off die manich
feldige clage des hantbergks der becken und Stad
es is vil wol vor uns brocht haben wir die obgenanten
zeite un grosser undedenuge und zwetracht stunde

Above: **Ordinances issued by Louis XIV regarding the status of bakers in the Faubourg Saint-Germain in Paris, March 1659.**

all those we call the lower classes subsisted only on mixed barley and oat bread from which the bran was not even removed, so that you could lift some of these loaves by the oat straws that they contained." The historical records are full of still worse accounts. On May 30, 1631, the Duke of Orléans wrote to his brother, the king: "Some of your subjects, in the countryside, are dying of hunger, while others survive only on acorns, on grass, like animals, and even the most fortunate among them live only on bran and on blood salvaged from slaughterhouse drains." But it was during periods of war or seige that the lack of bread inspired the wildest notions. The siege of Paris by Henry IV during the summer of 1590 caused a horrifying famine, with a severe shortage of bread and a great many deaths. In his *Histoire physique et morale de Paris (Physical and Moral History of Paris),* Dulaure writes: "In the houses of the rich,

people nourished themselves with bread made of oat flour. The poor devised a way of pulverizing slate to make a sort of bread from it. They went even further—they unearthed bones in graveyards. These bones, reduced to powder, formed a dish known as the 'bread of Madame de Montpensier'." Such extreme measures are stark indicators of the vital, almost obsessive role that bread played in the daily diet then.

Black Bread, White Bread

Bread is not only a quite logical symbol of social hierarchy, but also a revealing indicator of inequalities. For poor peasants there was a meager subsistence bread of mixed flours and herbs, berries, and crushed roots, whereas for city folk, superior bread and a more varied diet were available—in the sixteenth century, meat consumption increased from 20 kg to 40 kg per person per year.

Good King Henry and the Bakers

Henry IV passionately loved the *jeu de paume*, which was then at the height of its popularity. On Friday March 16, 1590, according to the chronicler Pierre de l'Estoile, the king, having taken the city of Mantes and looking for some entertainment, played a game of *paume* against bakers from the town "who won his money and refused a rematch, claiming that they had played a game with no return match. Much annoyed by this setback and furious at having consorted with such ill-bred people, Henry decided to be avenged, even if in a less than royal way: the next day, on his order, the town crier announced throughout the city that the price of a small loaf had been reduced by one *carolus* to a total of two *liards*. After which, the bakers, much distraught, came to beg his Majesty to take pity on them and have his revenge any way he pleased as long as it was not upon their bread."

Below: **The siege of Mantes-la-Jolie by Henry IV, in 1590.**

Denouncing the "Flour-Heads"

Flour-based cosmetic powder, widely used on wigs and hair in the seventeenth and eighteenth centuries, was prohibited several times during periods of famine. Voltaire himself denounced "the money that the most fashionable part of the nation spends on fine flour to powder its head."

A 1645 pamphlet entitled *Reproches des coquettes de Paris aux en-farinés sur la cherté du pain (Reproaches from Parisian Coquettes to Flour-Heads Concerning the High Cost of Bread)* satirized those laughable fops, perceived symbolically—but not without exaggeration—as exploiters of the starving masses: "Gentlemen, know ye that you are the ones who may be fairly accused of the high cost of bread, as you have cravenly profaned the uses of flour by turning it into a bodily adornment rather than a nourishing substance. Yes, your hair has squandered more of it than your mouth, and you have allowed your coat collars to eat up more of it in one day than you would use in one month to feed yourselves. Pernicious custom and cursed purpose of lovesick old men who have found no better way to appear younger than to drag others into old age with them; and who, in order to conceal the flaws of their years, which are never so betrayed as by the whiteness of the hair, have devised a way to render this color alluring in the eyes of the young so that they will feel imperfect."

The author then promises the worst punishments for those who persist in their bad habit: "If henceforth your hair is still floured, we will send you gleaning so you can have your flour; we will send you to work for bakers and masons since you like their color; and as the ultimate misfortune, once you have sold your finery out of urgent need, we will send you to the old clothes dealers where you can scrape what little flour remains all mixed with grease, so that you can make yourselves a little treat . . ."

Yesterday, February 22, I went to the House of Peers. It was a beautiful day, very cold in spite of the sun and the noon hour. On the Rue de Tournon, I saw a man being taken away by two soldiers. He was blond, pale, thin, haggard, about thirty years old, wearing coarse trousers, his feet bare and scraped in clogs with bloody rags wrapped around his ankles by way of hose, dressed in a short shirt with the back all muddy, showing that he usually slept on the pavement, his head bare and his hair all tangled. He had a loaf of bread under his arm. People around him were saying that he had stolen this bread and that this was why he was being taken away.

(Victor Hugo, *Choses vues 1830–1846,* year 1846)

All sorts of excesses were possible, as evidenced by a royal ordinance concerning a certain "Baker to the Little White Dogs." In 1546, this position—which probably did not outlast the reign of Henry II (1519–1559)—was bestowed upon the baker Antoine Andrault, purveyor of special little rolls to the king's favorite dogs. (For the record, even a century later, the ten *setiers* of mixed grain that a Paris laborer needed in order to feed his family, represented more than half his salary.)

In Italy during the seventeenth and eighteenth centuries, white bread was still a luxury. Just as in Roman times, hard wheat *(forte)* predominated (4 to 6 times more wheat than barley): it was eaten by the poor as black bread, 95% sifted and barely separated from waste and shell. Since the 1500s, rich city dwellers had been eating soft wheat *(maiorca, rocella),* 70 to 75% sifted, producing a bread as white as the one we know today. As for hard wheat noodles, although available since the thirteenth century, they remained a luxury until the eighteenth century—they were eaten sweet and were considered a dessert. Pound for pound, they cost three times as much as bread in 1600 and still twice as much in 1700. Year in and year out, the average daily ration of a French peasant was 800 grams of bread (half rye, half wheat), according to *La Dîme royale (The Royal Tithe),* a work published anonymously in 1707 by the elderly Maréchal Vauban (and later slated by Louis XIV's Royal Council for destruction by pulping). In sixteenth-century Poland, the average ration of an agricultural worker was 920 grams per day; in Italy, during the same period, this ration amounted to about 600 grams of black bread for an adult. The salary of a Sicilian agricultural worker, which did not change from 1400 to 1900, was 1.3 kg to 2 kg of bread per day, with which he had to feed his entire family. Monks seemed to fare better, particularly in the Benedictine order: chapter 39 of the *Règle de Saint Benoît (Rule of Saint Benedict),* devoted to food allotment, states that "a fully weighed pound of bread will serve for the day." As it happens, the Saint Benedict pound standard which has been preserved at Mont-Cassin is equal to 1,050 of our modern grams.

The Era of Monopolies

The famines which succeeded each other with almost mathematical regularity—1643, 1659, 1661–62, 1683, 1693, and 1709 were all calamitous years in France—were marked by sporadic peasant revolts, always individual or localized.

Left: **Francisco de Zurbarán,
*Saint Hugh in the
Refectory Blesses Food
Served to Charterhouse
Brothers,* 1633.**

The "Miller of Barbaste"

"His Majesty did dine, sup and retire in the fields." So reads one entry in the chronicles of the Maison du Béarnais, relating the adventurous life, dappled with innumerable peasant anecdotes, of Good King Henry in Gascony.

On the road from Agen to Nérac, Henry IV liked to indulge in long deer hunts, then stop at the fortified Barbaste mill high above the Gélise river, to dine with the local host. This time-honored custom earned him the nickname of Miller of Barbaste, as it had for his father, and he accepted it with pleasure. This familiarity, this free and easy attitude on the part of the prince, his way of honoring the villager's table, were well received by the people—or so the legend goes.

The same royal chronicles are even more verbose about the sometimes Rabelaisian nature of those meals, even if historical painting reflects a less faithful account, as in the Alexandre Menjaud canvas illustrated here, with its concern for "sober" hagiography. Bread was featured at these celebrations, as we can see, even if its presence in this depiction was minimal:

"Saturday October 6, 1576: dinner at Barbaste, retired at Nérac. 58 dozen loaves of bread, 4 barrels of wine, 1 dozen bottles, 8 x 20 *livres* of beef, 213 *livres* of mutton, 94 *livres* of veal, 26 capons, 76 chickens, pigeons, and grouse, 4 partridges, 5 rabbits, 2 young hares, 12 little game birds, 4 dishes of beef tripe, 4 mutton bellies, 1 dozen sausages, 2 *quarterons* of eggs (50 eggs), 42 *livres* of lard, 4 pigeon pasties, 14 baked pieces (pastries), fruit, etc."

However, it should be remembered that the king had a large entourage.

A child stealing a loaf of bread would be sentenced to serve on the galleys for life: one hundred thousand convicts were sent to man the king's ships between 1685 and 1749.

The situation worsened in 1729, when a private company was awarded a monopoly in grain trading in France, causing prices to rise. For, as became evident, a good harvest did not necessarily guarantee that bread would be available. Resellers and hoarders struck deals with the grain merchants, arriving at the markets before they were officially open to pick up grain for later resale at excessive prices. Other restrictive practices became common: if a harvest promised to be excellent, as in 1694, wheat merchants or loan sharks would corner the market, thus gaining control of the crop and its relevant prices. The cost of wheat would then increase overnight.

Bakers were routinely accused of exploiting every scarcity, whether genuine or not, and of spreading the most alarming stories in order to raise the price of bread. Their profession at the center of a subsistence network made them negative targets for public opinion, which tarnished them with a robber mentality—along with millers—and suspected them, rightly or wrongly, of exploiting the misery of the poor. "One hundred bakers, one hundred millers, and one hundred tailors make three hundred thieves," as the Dutch saying goes.

It was certainly easy to commit fraud, either by cheating on the weight of bread or by buying contaminated grain or flour at a low price for blending. But penalties were heavy: in 1690 for instance, when the previous year's poor harvest had further increased the cost of wheat, a certain Pasquier, found guilty of using spoiled flour, "was sentenced to a fine of 500 pounds, with his oven to be destroyed and his business to remain closed for six months"—not to mention a suspended sentence of corporal punishment if there were to be a repeat offense.

Left: **Bread shortage during the Revolution. Gouache by Lesueur.**

BREAD OF THE REVOLUTION

According to Fernand Braudel's succinct formulation, "the trinity: wheat, flour, bread, permeates the history of Europe. It is the main concern of cities, of states, of merchants, of people for whom to live has meant 'to bite into the bread.' In the correspondence of the time, bread was a recurring, dominant presence." Precisely because it became impossible to bite into one's bread, events in France accelerated toward the breaking point.

On the eve of the Revolution, nearly all conditions were ripe for the population's anger to explode. The crisis in French agriculture continued through the reigns of Louis XIV and Louis XVI; yields remained inferior, with six grains harvested for one seed planted (compared to eleven or twelve to one in Belgian Flanders), and crops remained largely insufficient. In 1765, the price of bread tripled. In his *Tableau de Paris,* Louis-Sébastien Mercier wrote in 1770 as a concerned and observant witness of those troubled times: "This will be the third winter in a row that bread is expensive. Half of the peasants needed public charity last year, and this winter will be the last straw, as those who survived until now by selling their belongings have nothing left to sell." Five years later, in the midst of another crisis, and contrary to the anticipated effect of a free market for grain decreed by Turgot, the price of bread in Paris increased from 8 *sous* to 14 *sous.* This sudden rise in price triggered the "flour war" during which bakeries were looted and transportation boats attacked on the Seine. Any grain traffic was interpreted as deliberate speculation to "starve the people." Then, after a major summer drought followed by a harsh winter, prices reached their peak in 1788–89: wheat was never more expensive than in May 1789, and hunger riots spread throughout France.

On July 6, Jacques Necker—recalled to the finance ministry—announced that rye would be used in order to save wheat, and that it would even be served at the royal table. But Paris had no bread: at the Bastille, people were hunting for flour rather than for prisoners. Behind the Versailles palace gates, Marie-Antoinette, hearing the demonstrators clamoring for bread, is said to have uttered her spontaneous and now famous remark: "If they have no more bread, let them eat cake!" On October 5, the Parisians returned to Versailles to bring back "the baker, the baker's wife, and the little doughboy," meaning the king, the queen, and the dauphin. But bread remained just as scarce after the royal family's return to Paris: bakeries were attacked and looted, bakers were beaten. The citizens were in a blind fury. On September 15, 1789, while wheat was being unloaded at a bakery on Rue du Faubourg-Saint-Martin, a sack full of sweepings burst open. According to eyewitness accounts describing the incident, the people in the crowd became murderous, thinking that they would be expected to eat spoiled flour, and they were just about ready to hang the culprit. It was only thanks to the intervention of a National Guard captain, who harangued the crowd and blocked the doorway, that the baker's life was saved. Other bakers were less fortunate, including one found to have stashed a quantity of loaves in his basement, concealed under a woodpile. The furious populace seized him, hanged him from a lamp post, cut off his head, and then paraded it impaled on a pike through Paris—in the best revolutionary tradition—before returning it to his terrorized wife in a gesture of ultimate cruelty. Bread was not to be taken lightly, and mob justice was there to serve as a reminder.

On July 19, 1791, the Constituent Assembly set mandatory prices for bread, and at the end of 1792, the National Convention decreed that bakers could bake only one kind of bread, *pain d'égalité,* the egalitarian bread, from a blend of ¾ wheat and ¼ rye, including the bran. White flour was prohibited. On December 12, 1793, the Convention introduced a universal rationing card, *carte de pain,* allotting "one and a half *livres* for workers and heads of families, one livre for others."

The Revolution had come to an end, but the questions about bread remained.

The "Flour War"

The Flour War broke out on April 18, 1775, in Dijon on a market day. A rich miller suspected of mixing bean flour into wheat flour was called to account by the crowd. His house and mill were sacked. Similar events occurred in Beaumont-sur-Oise on April 27 and in Pontoise on April 29. Merchants and millers were robbed and sometimes attacked. The same anger erupted everywhere: flour was too expensive, often of poor quality, and it made bread unaffordable.

At dawn on May 2, peasants marched on Versailles and mobbed the castle gates; the military governor took it upon himself to announce that the king had agreed to lower the price of bread. Louis XVI called this "a foolish action" and sent a note to Turgot, general finance comptroller, saying: "You can count on my firmness. I have just sent the guards marching to the market." The crowd dispersed without any resistance but soon realized it had been duped: bread stayed at 14 *sous*.

The next day, the Flour War reached Paris, as reported by police commissioner Lenoir: "On May 3, 1775, between seven and nine in the morning, I received the first warning that a substantial number of peasants had been seen crossing at the barriers, but that they were almost all carrying vegetables and asparagus and seemed interested only in selling their goods. I was also informed about a disturbance that had started at the Bread Market." The first skirmishes occurred when soldiers forbade access to the Market. The disorder soon spread to other neighborhoods. Breaking down the bakers' doors, the rioters forced them to sell bread at low prices, under the indifferent gaze of the archers standing guard. The situation deteriorated with the looting of bread and flour or even money from the bakers' tills. But only a few dozen of the thousand bakeries in Paris were actually looted. Lenoir comments further: "This looting was rather peculiar: it was carried out without much violence and it has been noted that pastry shops remained open and that their displays were respected through that whole day." These seem to have been less ferocious rioters than those described by Voltaire in his pamphlet, when he writes of "the horrors committed by this horde," and says that the demonstrators "were all drunk and shouting all the while that they were starving to death." The Parisians were not deceived, however, and watched the demonstrators with some amusement. The rioters brandished chunks of moldy bread under Turgot's windows, shouting: "Look! This is the bread they make us pay 14 *sous* for! It's poison!" Insults and jeers were rife, but there was no bloodshed. The commotion abated in the afternoon when musketeers appeared on the scene, sent from Versailles. In accordance with Turgot's orders, two soldiers were now posted in front of each bakery. By seven that evening, the last of the mob had dispersed. Among some one hundred people arrested was Abbé Saurin, author of *Réflexions d'un citoyen sur le commerce des grains (Reflections of a Citizen on the Grain Trade),* which took a hostile view of Turgot's liberalism. Two of the rioters, wigmaker Jean-Denis Desportes and an apprenticed worker, Jean-Charles L'Eguiller, were hanged a week later on the Place de Grève to serve as examples. The uprising was over.

This irrational and unpredictable Flour War was a forerunner of what was to come in 1789 and served, in its way, as a tragi-comic rehearsal of the French Revolution.

Left: **Distribution of bread at the Louvre during the 1709 famine. Nineteenth-century engraving.**

MODERN TIMES

Democratic Dreams

Hardly anything seemed likely to resolve them in the next century: neither mechanization, nor the increasingly convenient channels of communication, nor the progress of agronomy (the first high-yield, insect and climate resistant wheat hybrids did not appear until early in the twentieth century), nor even the potato, although its cultivation would later precipitate a true food-crop revolution in these grain-oriented cultures. In 1846 for instance, a disastrous harvest suddenly raised the price of bread and caused a certain amount of unrest throughout France: 635,000 Parisians out of a population of 900,000 required assistance. The following year, 394,000 were still receiving bread or special cards to get it more cheaply.

The course of the nineteenth century alternated between regulation and deregulation, taxes and exemptions, authoritarian and liberal measures, according to the will of the current political regime. Judging by the profusion of protests in the press and in pamphlets against its rising price, bread remained a basic necessity. Throughout the century, the color of bread became more than ever a sign of its consumer's upward mobility. Bran bread was the bread of the poor, those who had nothing. White bread, with all its connotations of prestige and luxury, was for the leaders, for the bourgeoisie. Flour was washed and sifted to the limit, so that all its nutritional value and vitamins were lost. Black bread was like nature, with all its imperfections and torments.

Until the end of the century, bread remained the highly symbolic subject of many speculations and utopias. In February 1896, some two thousand years after the Romans, a certain Clovis Hugues, a representative of the nineteenth district of Paris, introduced a draft of a law requiring bakers to distribute free bread to the public; the municipalities would reimburse the bakers from a special fund raised through additional penny-tax contributions. Needless to say, his measure was declared farfetched or ruinous, and fell into oblivion.

Bread as Utopia?

Riots generated by hunger have not vanished from the world: in many Third World countries, bread is currently subsidized, which may be helpful to city dwellers but is not always in the interest of the farmers. Various attempts to raise the price of bread, often in compliance with International Monetary Fund directives, have regularly triggered social unrest or demonstrations, such as the ones in Poland and Romania (1981), Tunisia (1984), Jordan, and Russia—where the cost of bread tripled in 1990. In the Ukraine, bread became seven times more expensive in 1994, and in 1996, Jordan's king had to ask his government to reduce the price of bread, whose 250% increase had triggered disturbances.

At the dawn of the third millennium, trying to feed the world's entire population still remains a somewhat utopian endeavor.

Opposite: **A World War I footsoldier eating a meal of dry bread. Autochrome by Paul Castelnau, 1917.**

Pages 52–53: **Emile Friant, *Boaters on the Meurthe*, 1887.**

Below: **In 1945, bread was even scarcer in France than it had been during the war. Coupons provided only inadequate rations. Here, Parisians wait in line in front of a bakery.**

51

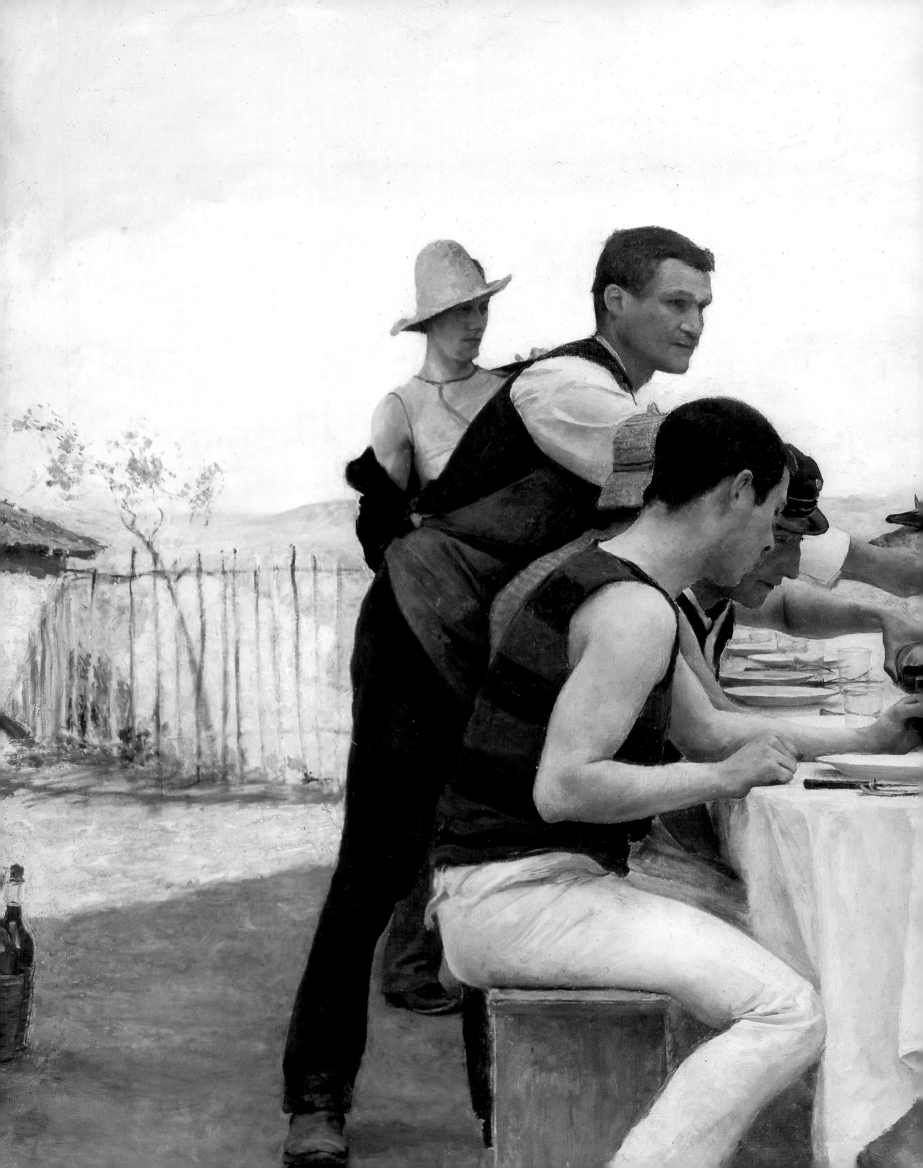

MODERN BAKERY

Visitors to the 1867 Universal Exposition in Paris greeted its innovations with a mixture of curiosity and skepticism. People had not forgotten the failure of the first wooden dough mixers introduced in the waning years of the eighteenth century and operated with a crank. And how about the eighteen-horsepower steam-driven device capable of operating four mixers at the same time? Beyond its technical prowess, this large-scale industrial approach to the baker's trade was not well received: during the Second Empire, only about twenty of these steam mixers were installed in France, and their owners found that they had made a bad investment. Paradoxically, under that regime's official semi-liberalism, industrial baking projects remained surprisingly few. Here and there, a small milling and bread-making operation survived, with difficulty. There were also a few attempts to establish cooperatives—not as a result of any bakers' initiative but instead spearheaded by associations, such as the one organized by the

Chemin de Fer d'Orléans for its employees in 1868, or the Grenelle and Vaugirard Consumer Cooperative actually established by wine merchants. But none lasted very long. Only the Scipion bakery—named after the former owner of the building, Scipion Sardini, a gentleman from Lucca, who had come to France with Marie de Médicis and whose townhouse became the General Hospital's official bakery in 1675—owned ten mechanical mixers driven by a ten-horsepower steam engine. In addition to supplying the markets, this bakery provided bread to all Second Empire public welfare establishments, as well as the fire departments and the seminaries of Paris (the type of enterprise, in other words, that was anathema to traditional bakers). In France, followers of the artisanal traditions of bread-making, unlike those in the milling trade, resisted industrial concentration and the cooperative movement. There was a strong and continuing resistance from bakers and craftsmen in the trade, for whom the art of kneading dough —hand kneading—remained the essence of the craft; and resistance, as well, from the consumer, who could only view this "mechanized bread" with a distinct sense of uneasiness.

Bread and Machines

Adaptation to the new methods took time in Europe, and particularly in France. The trade today is very different. Professional baking had been too arduous. It had meant working all night before the demanding early morning customers arrived. Hand kneading, in particular, was a strenuous task. In addition, journeyman workers were poorly paid for far too many working hours (up to sixteen-hour days!), and no other business stays open from 6:30 in the morning until 8:30 at night.

Taxes on the price of bread impeded the improvement of working conditions. As a result, small bakery owners were forced to mechanize or go out of business. Automatic ovens, fast-rising yeasts, and mechanical mixers came into general

Below: **One of the earliest mechanized bakeries in Paris, 1885.**

Above: **An innovation
in 1900: steam-driven
mobile bakeries.**

use during the 1920s, and high-speed mixers have been widely available since 1956.

But this "modern" dough was so over-handled, forced, mistreated, oxygenated into whiteness, frozen, and reheated, that bread took its revenge: it became white, dull, without texture or substance, seemingly containing nothing more than water and air, like those baguettes already stale, brittle, or gummy just three hours after purchase. Such was the sad state to which bread had been reduced in the 1960s.

Fortunately, those days are past. That mushy, dry, tasteless bread has practically disappeared, not only in artisanal bakeries, but to a large extent in industrial bakeries as well. Experience and tradition have been able to withstand the modernist avalanche that assaulted the baking world, with its automated operations and its barbaric vocabulary: proportioners, rounders, dividers, weighers,

molders, fast beaters; controlled fermentation chambers, freezers, heating tables, bread scarifiers, continuous rollers, automatic preparation and finishing lines, automatic coating machines; slicers, wrappers, baggers, automated bread-making lines and regulators, and so on.

Yet today, not all French bakers produce good bread. The standard quality of bread could still be improved, a shortcoming that has often contributed to the public's increasing alienation: the average daily consumption of bread in France dropped from 600 grams in 1900 to 170 grams in 1992.

Flour quality is certainly excellent and very carefully controlled, but it has been standardized —along with wheat varieties—to the point that bread too often tastes the same everywhere. Everything is mixed and sent to the mill to ensure a consistent quality. High-speed kneading doubles the volume of the bread by incorporating a large

amount of air. The flour must then be corrected with the three additives that are allowed in France: bean flour (2% maximum) added at the mill to speed the oxidation of the dough and whiten it; wheat malt or barley flour (0.3% maximum) to improve the fermentation of flour with low sugar content; and ascorbic acid (0.003% maximum) to increase the dough's cohesiveness and strength.

Industrial Bakeries

Industrial bakeries have operated in France since 1959, following the already well-established example of the United States. They were introduced there in 1849 by W. B. Ward, whose enterprises expanded rapidly until 1924, when his Continental Baking Company acquired the General Baking Corporation, thus creating a genuine bakery cartel. In England, this industry was established in the 1870s, improving upon the miserable sanitation and working conditions common in small bakeries—prepackaged industrial bread now supplies 75% of England's consumption.

France now has about 200 industrial bakeries, four or five of which are truly significant

Above: **At the beginning of the twentieth century in Paris, handcarts deliver the first loaves of bread produced by non-artisan bakeries.**

(the Pain Jacquet company controls 35% of the sandwich bread market). These enterprises employ about 10,000 people, supplying mainly collectivities and supermarkets; they account for 30% of total bread consumption (3% thirty years ago). Some of them manufacture prepackaged products (sandwich loaves) that cannot be made by the artisanal bakeries, and others mass-produce baguettes.

Even so, industrial bakeries in France complain about competition from prepackaged bread imported from Germany or England, despite the fact that those products fail to conform to the very strict French regulations regarding food additives. Manufacturers must add preservatives such as propionic acid (E280, 281, 282), which acts as a mold inhibitor and protects sandwich bread and packaged loaves, while the flour is artificially whitened. The unfortunate popularity of white bread requires the elimination of bran, and therefore of gluten, proteins, and wheat germ. While white bread may keep longer than whole grain bread, brown bread—which retains the bran—is healthier.

Industrial bakeries are incontestably dynamic. They know how to raise capital, launch new products, attract franchises, and market their innovations. Their expansion is to be expected in an era of standardization in which finance and capital predominate. Distribution chains are emerging just about everywhere, baking industrially prepared frozen lumps of dough at points of sale in prime urban locations. Brioches and croissants are baked in subway stations nowadays, in shops called *Points Chauds, Brioche Dorée,* or *Croissanterie.* Chains are opening branches overseas, in Japan *(Ganachaud)* or in the United States (*Croissant Show, Brioche Dorée, le Moulin de la Vierge,* and so on).

Bread, which has been a universal food, has now become a global product.

Below: **Bread-making in one of the earliest industrial bakeries of Germany, early twentieth century.**

FROM GRAIN TO BREAD

From what a poet has called the noble gesture of the sower, much work remains to be done before the emergence of the hot fragrant bread! Bread production requires numerous steps: sowing and cultivating, followed by the harvest season; the grain is then sorted from its straw and husk, after which it is transformed into flour by increasingly sophisticated mills. Unleavened flatbreads are baked on hot slabs or stones. Leavened bread, lighter and more digestible thanks to the use of starter or yeast, must be baked in ovens, whose structure may vary within different cultural contexts. Then as now, the cycle of bread production has remained lengthy and complex, yet in spite of mechanical progress and a degree of labor automation, it has retained all of its nobility.

Left: **Donkeys carry wheat after harvesting. Karpathos Island, Greece.**

Opposite: **Wheat stalks gathered by hand near Briançon.**

BREAD WITHOUT GRAINS

Overly accustomed as we have become to white bread, we tend to associate bread exclusively with wheat, or perhaps with rye, which is the bread often eaten with oysters. But until recently, wheat has actually been a very secondary grain. In the past, rather than wheat, people ate barley, millet, oats, buckwheat, maize, sorghum, manioc, or rye. Some cultures were unaware of the very existence of grains. The people of Melanesia ate tubers or gruels of fermented taro packed into sealed lengths of bamboo and roasted in ashes. And in New Guinea, sago palm gatherers still prepare a fermented mash with the starch extracted from these trees.

The Indians' Cassava

The Indians of South America have always eaten starch extracted from the cassava root. Originally, cassava, or manioc, was probably cultivated in the tropical forest of Eastern Venezuela. Later, it became more widespread in the Americas, starting in Colombia where it is called yucca. There are two kinds of cassava: sweet manioc, which can be eaten raw or cooked, and bitter manioc, whose bulky yellowish root is prized for its high starch content. But when fresh, this starch contains hydrogen cyanide, or prussic acid, which must be removed before it can be used as food. To this end, the Indians pack the grated manioc into a long tube fashioned from diagonally braided liana fibers (for high elasticity), and compress it to force out the poisonous juice.

The dough obtained from coarse manioc flour is spread on a large pottery slab whose diameter can reach sixty centimeters, and which is set on the fire. This yields a flat cake which can be stored and used for barter. Eaten hot, it has a nice almond and hazelnut flavor, although it is thick and still doughy inside. When cold, it is reheated before eating.

The Potato or "Poor Man's Bread"

The potato, *Solanum tuberosa,* provides the only serious competition to the daily consumption of rye or wheat bread in Europe. From an equal area of cultivation, it can feed five times more people than wheat.

Originally cultivated by the Incas and brought back to Europe from Peru in about 1550, this small tuber was first cultivated in Spain and then Italy. It was, above all, via England, where Walter Raleigh introduced it in 1585, that the potato became known throughout Europe. But it had a rather bad reputation. Long considered a botanical curiosity—in 1616, it was served as an exotic novelty at the table of King Louis XIII —and later used as cattle feed or as a bread of last resort, the potato was most widespread in Ireland, Flanders, Lorraine, the Vosges, and the Netherlands, and it was still viewed with suspicion on the eve of the Revolution. It was criticized for having a multitude of flaws. Doctors blamed it for spreading leprosy, scrofula, and all types of fevers. Economists did not like it much better because it upset their theories. And Diderot's *Encyclopedia* found fault with it for being "wind-breaking." There was virtually nothing for which it was not blamed.

Antoine Augustin Parmentier (1737–1813) discovered its nutritional value when he was imprisoned near Hanover during the Seven Years' War (1756–1763), in which he had served as an assistant pharmacist. From then on, Parmentier never ceased to promote this tuber.

Named apothecary-major at the Hôtel des Invalides in 1772, he published his *Examen chimique des pommes de terre (Chemical Analysis of the Potato)* in 1774, working all the while to improve bread-making techniques. On October 29, 1777, Parmentier and a pharmacist-chemist, Cadet de Vaux, organized a baking demonstration at the Invalides, using potato flour. He also experimented with corn, chestnut, Jerusalem artichoke, and sweet potato flours mixed with rye or wheat. The following year, he published a book at the Imprimerie Royale which became a standard reference: *Le parfait boulanger, ou traité complet sur la fabrication et le commerce du pain (The Perfect Baker; Complete Treatise on Bread-making and Marketing).*

Opposite: **Pounding cassava meal. Ivory Coast.**

Below: **Potato market. Uzbekistan.**

The "Economy Bread" of Antoine-Augustin Parmentier

I n 1771, the Academy of Besançon initiated a competition based on the following subject: "Indicate the vegetal substances, which in times of famine, might replace those that commonly feed mankind . . ." Antoine-Auguste Parmentier, who was then an assistant apothecary to the armed services, won the first prize. In his essay, he demonstrated that the most nutritious of all vegetable substances is starch, and showed how it is possible to convert this starch, particularly potato starch, into bread that is fit to eat.

He was neither the first nor the only person to study the conversion of this tuber into a bread-making substance. Fulguet had already introduced a potato bread in 1761; the chemist Guillaume-François Rouelle had also studied it, as had François-Georges Mustel, author of *Mémoire sur les pommes de terre et le pain économique, 1767 (Essay on the Potato and on Economy Bread).*

Below: *Antoine Augustin Parmentier* (1737–1813), portrait by Quenedey. This army pharmacist introduced the potato into French cooking.

But Parmentier devoted himself to promoting the potato with quasi-religious fervor. Delegates from the Academy of Sciences were invited to taste this already famous bread. Did the tasting committee have a jaded palate that day? Were there unrealistic expectations for this miracle bread? Rumor has it that these gentlemen did not find it to be quite as advertised. Here and there, voices were raised in derision of Parmentier and his supporters, who found themselves nicknamed "potatomaniacs." An anonymous 1780 pamphlet entitled *Jugement impartial et sério-comi-critique d'un manant, cultivateur & bailli de son village, sur le pain de pomme de terre pure (An Impartial, Serio-Comic-Critical Judgment from a Villager, Farmer, and Village Bailiff, Concerning Pure Potato Bread),* waxes ironic about those who attempt "to establish that it is possible to make a pure potato bread as tasty, as pleasant, as nourishing—in a word as perfect—as the best of wheat bread, & at a lower price."

Potatoes alone are too starchy for breadmaking. Parmentier acknowledges in his *Traité de boulangerie (Treatise on Baking)* that his "attempts to convert potatoes into bread without adding flour have had absolutely no success. Nor can one succeed with potatoes that have been dried in the oven, powdered, & blended with their pulp. The bread thus obtained is absolutely worthless."

Opposite: **Parmentier, attempting to interest Louis XVI in his experimental potato bread after the 1785 famine, offers the King a bouquet of potato flowers.**

But the agronomist-chemist did not give up. Once the potato was mixed with secondary flours which, on their own, would never produce anything but mediocre bread, it finally became possible to produce "good bread," that would have particular flavor qualities: with the addition of potatoes, barley lost its harshness, Turkish wheat its dryness, buckwheat its bitterness. Nevertheless, the bread-making method that Parmentier advocated was impractical on a large scale. Detractors pointed out that potato peeling, in particular, was a time-consuming operation which obviated any notion of economy; they also said that this bread was less nourishing and that you had to eat more of it than bread made from other kinds of flour; but the clinching argument was that, since people ate potatoes anyway, why bother to make bread out of them?

The sole and undeniable benefit of bread made with potato flour was that it would keep for over a year without molding or excessive hardening. Its advantages were debated for a time among royal agricultural societies as a possible substitute for the *biscuit* rations issued to the armies and navies. But the topic faded away.

On June 8, 1780, together with Cadet de Vaux and Paris Police Lieutenant Lenoir, he opened the School of Bakery on Rue de la Grande Truanderie. The courses, which were free, came to an end before the Revolution. In 1786, with royal permission, he cultivated potatoes on the grounds at les Sablons in Neuilly. On August 24, at Versailles, he offered a bouquet of blooming potato stalks to King Louis XVI, who adorned his buttonhole and the queen's hat with them, thus starting a fad for the plant, which became known as the "royal orange."

Parmentier understood that the potato (which contains too much starch) would never become widely accepted through bread-making, but rather through the development of appropriate cooking methods. On October 24, 1787, his sister Marie-Suzanne served steamed potatoes at another dinner at the Invalides, described by an English traveler, Arthur Young, in his book published in London in 1792.

In the nineteenth century, the potato, then known almost everywhere in France as the "poor man's bread," was to bring about a veritable agricultural revolution in our grain-oriented societies. As in the case of bread, potato consumption in France has decreased in recent times, from 178 kg per person per year in 1925 to 140 kg in 1935 and 70 kg today.

Chestnuts

Parmentier also attempted to improve the bread-making properties of chestnut flour. In some parts of central France, neither wheat nor potatoes would replace chestnut bread until the beginning of the twentieth century. In Corsica, the chestnut tree is called a "bread tree" and chestnut flour is still a staple. In 1996, some bold entrepreneurs launched a Corsican beer, the Pietra brand, brewed from chestnut flour and malt.

Soybeans

So rich in proteins that they can be used to replace meat, soybeans also contain mineral salts and vitamins. Soy flour has no gluten and so cannot be used for bread. But the addition of 5% soy flour to wheat flour will double the protein content. Americans regularly include 5 to 10% soy

flour in their bread. The United States is the leading producer of soybeans, massive quantities of which are exported to Europe for cattle feed.

Rice

By itself, rice flour is not well suited to bread-making, but it is possible to incorporate up to 15% of it into wheat flour without significantly altering the appearance and flavor of the bread. Rice was widely used in Venice during periods of famine, and as late as 1926, the Italian Ministry of National decreed the addition of 5% rice flour to wheat flour—an adjunct which is prohibited in France.

Above: **Wheat threshing floor. China.**

Pages 64–65: **Harvested field. Abruzzi region, Italy.**

THE MAJOR GRAINS

There is no true bread without grains and there is no well-risen bread without grains containing enough gluten so that the water and flour dough, which constitutes bread in the strict sense of the word, will produce a solid and resilient loaf after being kneaded, fermented, and baked. This is the requirement that accounts for the primacy of the various kinds of wheat and rye among breadmaking grains. Our culture's main grains, its wheats, ryes, and barleys, all belong to the same group, the *Triticales* or *Hordea* in the *Gramineae* family. All were well represented in the native meadows of the Near East where pre-Neolithic gatherers found their "wild" grains.

Our modern varieties are the descendants of these native grains, highly modified and "improved" through human selection. This is notably the case with hexaploid wheat or *Triticum aesti-*

vum, var. *aestivum,* which is the source of today's most desirable baking flour, while the tetraploid, *Triticum turgidum,* var. *durum,* is the main basis of those flours used for making noodles.[3] Following the rise of bread-making, grains had diverse histories depending upon their properties.

Millet, cultivated since ancient times—some of this grain has been found in Switzerland's lake cities and in the pile dwellings of Italy's Lake Varese—was prevalent in Southern Europe. Although this grain is less nourishing than wheat or barley, it was sometimes used as an ingredient in bread. But it was reserved especially for animal feed because the stems and leaves of common millet make good cattle forage.

Although millet was grown in Europe until the seventeenth century, it can now be found only locally in France. It is still widely used in Africa,

Below: **Stalks of wheat, oats, and barley.**

Right: **Wheat winnowing.
Rajasthan, India.**

Opposite: **Gathering
wheat into sheaves.
Rajasthan, India.**

however, particularly in the Sahel region. It imparts a slight acidity and is still an ingredient in some multi-grain novelty breads; it is often mixed with wheat, the nobler grain.

Raw oats are a favorite fodder as a source of energy for horses everywhere, while the Scots and the Irish are among the last to have remained faithful to oat porridges and breads, prompting the famous moralist and lexicologist Samuel Johnson to include this rather dour definition in his *Dictionary of the English Language (1747–1755):* "Oats are known in Scotland as human food and in England as horse fodder."

Barley yields a heavy sort of bread unless mixed with wheat or rye. It is often used, however, to make flat cakes, as is cornmeal. At the time of Christ, the Palestinians ate barley bread, and we know that in Samaria, a measure of fine wheat flour was worth twice the same amount of barley.

Barley bread is still eaten in India, and in Tibet, where it is served with buttered tea.

Rustic and sturdy rye is perfectly suited to the soil and climate of Central Europe and Central Asia. It resists where wheat would freeze, and therefore plays a central role in the diet of those regions. Rye actually supplanted oats in eighteenth-century Germany. It outperforms all other grains in yield: weight for weight, one grain of rye produces more flour than one wheat kernel. Since it is low in gluten, rye produces a dense bread that keeps a long time.

"Black wheat" or buckwheat, originating in Asia, reached Europe only in the fifteenth century. Its flour makes very nourishing pancakes and crêpes, which once served as the staple diet in certain poor regions. Mountain peasants in seventeenth-century Poland used to cook buckwheat cakes, and Stendhal writes about "the part of Brittany that speaks *Breton* and lives on buckwheat cakes."

But it was wheat (in its early rustic form as spelt, whose small grain is not easily separated from the husk), that eventually prevailed in eighteenth-century Europe.

That is when wheat cultivation began to replace rye in France, although it did not overtake it until after 1850. Until that time, white bread was reserved for the nobility, then for city dwellers, while the peasantry had to be content with black bread, rye, barley, or *méteil* (a mixture of half rye, half wheat). In Egypt, just as in ancient Greece and Rome, the same income-based hierarchy can be found: wheat, rye, barley. Much of Italy has kept its fondness for very white bread, but some thirty years ago its mountain people still ate mainly *polenta,* which was originally not made of corn but of barley or chestnut mush.

Couscous, probably of Sudanese origin, is a semolina that is rolled and steamed; it is made from hard wheat grown in Italy and in Mediterranean countries. By extension, the name applies to the dish of meat and vegetables served with it.

Corn in the New World

Corn originated in the Americas and was brought back to Spain in 1493 by Christopher Columbus, who wrote in his journal on November 5, 1492, that ears of corn "taste good, and all the people in this country sustain themselves with it."

European corn cultivation was first attempted in Andalusia in 1535 with no great success. Corn was carried to Italy and Crete in the sixteenth century by the Venetian fleet, then spread to Turkey in mid-century, becoming known as *Turkey Wheat* when it was rediscovered in Europe. In the Lombardy markets of the seventeenth century, this "Turkish wheat" sold for half the price of wheat. In France, corn reached Toulouse in 1639 under the name of *Spanish millet* or *coarse millet*. In the meantime, Portuguese sailors had introduced it in the Indies, to Java in 1496, and to China in 1516. It then replaced sorghum in certain parts of Africa. The spread of corn during the eighteenth century can be tracked through the inroads of pellagra: this disease of poor populations whose diet consists exclusively of ground corn, results from a Niacin deficiency (a B vitamin).

Over three hundred corn varieties are currently cultivated worldwide in at least parts of the continents of America, Europe, Asia, and Africa. But it still has a bad reputation in some regions and is not widely used for human consumption except where it has traditionally been eaten, in Spain, Portugal, Italy, Turkey, and, of course, America. While corn bread is still popular in the United States, the American food industry has also managed to turn corn into a modern high-consumption product by flaking or puffing the kernels into cereals such as corn flakes and into popcorn.

In France, the Southwestern areas (Gascony, Guyenne, the Basque country, and Béarn) are the only regions where corn is eaten regularly in the form of pancakes or fritters called *cruchades,* 1.5 cm thick and 6 cm in diameter, first boiled and then pan-fried. But the peasants of a century ago still relied heavily on corn cakes or on a gruel called *mestura.* In the South of France, corn was known as "yellow flour," which was cooked into thick porridges *(gaudes)* and boiled gruels *(polenta),* or baked in the oven *(milliasse).* Corn flour was sometimes also added to wheat when making bread.

Romanian peasants, like their Italian counterparts, eat boiled corn or *mamaliga* (the rationing adopted in Romania in October 1981 allotted 30 kg of corn per person in addition to 150 kg of wheat for the year). In Western Asia, corn flour was mixed with wheat to make bread during famines. Poor peasants eat pure corn bread, which is quite fragrant and flavorful when it comes out of the oven, but pasty, tasteless, and difficult to digest the next day. In the Balkans, people still make flat cornbread and cheese loaves, the *bobotas,* baked in the oven: corn flour and water are mixed with oil, then with white goat cheese. There is also a sweet version, incorporating raisins instead of cheese.

Opposite: **Ears of corn drying in the sun before being sold. Koki, Cambodia.**

Below: **Maize in ancient Mexico. Detail from Diego Rivera's** *La Grande Tenochtitclan.*

THE FORTUNES OF WHEAT

Wheat, the royal and conquering grain, Mediterranean in its origins, is now cultivated throughout Europe and the countries bordering the Mediterranean, as well as in the Near East, India, and Northern China. It has become acclimated in Canada, the United States, Argentina, Chile, South Africa, and even Australia. Global wheat production is steadily increasing and has grown from 502 million tons in 1989 to 537 million tons in 1997.

Precisely because of its predominance, wheat has long been a misnomer for various human consumption grains: "major wheats" for wheat and rye, "minor wheats" for barley and oats.

Wheat varieties are innumerable and their archaic names indicate their geographical diversity: Flanders, Whittington, Talavera, Chiddam, Saumur, Hungarian White, richelle de Grignon,

If hedonistic city dwellers knew how much labor is expended in order to furnish bread, they would be appalled.

(Voltaire, *Dictionnaire philosophique*)

Fellemberg, Scottish Red, Blue Southern Russian, Sicilian Square, Cretan, Tuscan, Naples Bearded, velu de la Manche, poulard rouge d'Auvergne, Sainte-Hélène Giant, and godelle du Lyonnais.

To this day, dozens of new varieties are being developed each year from multiple genetic mutations in agronomical research laboratories, in order to obtain strains that are more resistant, better suited to a particular soil or climate, or that produce higher yields, while retaining good bread-making properties. Some of the current French varieties are Soissons or Sidéral, Thésée or Scipion.

Below: **Winnowing wheat stalks. Karpathos Island, Greece.**

Left: **Oxen threshing
wheat under their hooves.
Rajasthan, India.**

Threshing and Flailing

When it is ripe, the wheat must be harvested—formerly by sickle or scythe, then, thanks to the industrial revolution, by horse-drawn harvester, then by harvester-thresher, and now by the harvester-thresher-baler combine, the modern mechanical monster.

The harvested wheat must be threshed, or flailed, to separate the grains. With the newer varieties, each wheat cluster contains up to sixty grains of wheat. The Egyptians used to simply drive oxen or donkeys across the threshing floor, where their hooves would burst the sheaves and release the grain. This trampling method is still to be found in various parts of the Mediterranean basin and was practiced until recently in the South of France. Sometimes, the sheaves were just struck against a wooden block, this makeshift method being used to process small quantities or to avoid damaging the rye straw. But in certain rural areas of Thailand, for example, this is still the way rice is flailed.

The marvelous invention of the *tribulum,* in which two, four, or even six thick wooden boards are juxtaposed, curving upward in front and lined at the bottom with sharpened flint, was known throughout the Mediterranean basin and all the way to Iran, Bulgaria, and Portugal. This sort of threshing harrow is hitched to a pair of draft animals that pulls it round and round while the flint separates the grain. Such a device was often weighted down with stones, or by the team driver. The *tribulum* was already known in Rome under the name of *plostellum poenicum,* which would suggest an oriental origin, and it is also mentioned in the Bible *(Isaiah, XLI, 15).*

Once worn, the flint must be replaced. At the Konya market in Turkey, as a poignant survival of prehistory, it is still possible to buy cut flint by the kilo in the corner reserved for agricultural implements. These *tribulums,* here called *dögen,* are still widely used in central Anatolia; they are disappearing elsewhere, giving way to mechanization, and are beginning to turn up in antique shops.

> I feel so keenly that the history of people is like the history of wheat, if you are not sown on the earth to germinate, what difference does it make, you will be milled to become bread.
>
> (Vincent van Gogh)

The Harvest Bouquets

In earlier times, as the year progressed, there would be many anxious queries addressed to the heavens, together with blessings, thanksgivings, and magical offerings—all of which were intended to motivate the divinity to respond to the people's wishes and grant them an abundance of grain. Modern harvest bouquets and crosses, corn dollies, and skillfully woven geometric designs, still suggest the quasi-sacred nature of the harvest. These customs persist notably throughout the Mediterranean Basin. Braided from the last sheaves of the crop, these bouquets and figures are hung on walls or in doorways to attract happiness and prosperity.

Such good luck charms are kept until the following harvest; their seeds are most likely scattered in the fields. Their designs are remarkably constant wherever they are found: in Italy, Greece, or England, horns of plenty spilling out sheaves; circular crowns in Yugoslavia, oval ones in Morocco where they are displayed horizontally (like the magic eye symbol of the Near East). In Yugoslavia, Bulgaria, Turkey, Egypt, or North Africa, there may be a rectangle enclosing a triangle from which hangs a bundle of wheat (the triangle, another eye symbol, brings fertility and protection against misfortune). In Sweden, peasants sometimes braid figures of their cattle, as if also seeking some form of magical protection.

The symbolism of the harvest bouquet has often been forgotten, but the custom remains of hanging a bouquet of wheat stalks as a beautiful decorative element inside the home or in shop windows.

Harvest bouquets woven from the crop's first wheat stalks.

Decorated breads eaten to celebrate the harvest's end (counterclockwise: Black Forest bread, Lunéville bread, Saint-Etienne bread).

The Harvest

In former times, the course of the year reflected an anxious expectation of the harvest, a day which would be blessed or cursed, depending upon the crop. For every good harvest, how many years of scarcity, of famine that seemed to signal the end of the world? Wheat has long ruled men's lives, determining their daily routine, even their very survival—sometimes to the point of obsession. For if wheat was wanting, all was wanting: flour, and with it bread, the heart of the meal in those days. It signified a state of serfdom, a blend of tenacity and resignation, worsened at times by dramatically unpredictable seasons: a spring frost that could prove fatal to young shoots, an excessively wet summer that would rot the grain, a storm that might obliterate in a few minutes the work of an entire year. Such is the amazing paradox that Louis-Sébastien Mercier notes with emotion as he reflects on eighteenth-century society: "The wheat which feeds man has also been his executioner."

Left: **Peter Brueghel the Younger,** *Summer,* 1620.
Ulm, Deutsches Brotmuseum.

The *tribulum* was sometimes replaced by a stone roller (in Southern and Southwestern France), or by a sled built of wood or willows weighted down with stones and hauled around the threshing floor by a team of oxen. In Roman times, this sled was known as the *plaustrum triturans*. In both Iran and Egypt, it was sometimes mounted on wooden wheels or circular iron blades that cut through the grain clusters.

Threshing with a flail, a traditional method in the humid regions of France, can be traced back to the fourth century A.D. It was carried out either in the open air after the harvest, or inside a barn in the winter.

The flail consists of a handle bound with a leather or eelskin strap to a thick short stick, or beater. In the Cévennes, where this technique was still practiced in the 1970s, the flail (or *fladjel*) had an ash handle and a beechwood beater, joined by two bull ligaments. Threshing would begin on August 15 and followed a tried-and-true technique: the sheaves would be spread out on the ground, with the grain clusters of the first layer facing inward and the next outward, so as to stabilize the whole. Two groups of three or four men facing one another would beat the clusters rhythmically. A team could thresh about one hundred sheaves in a half hour. But the favorite method, the best one for maintaining the rhythm, consisted of threshing in teams of three. In the Limousin, where threshing would last two weeks, the flail (called *fleu*) had an elderwood handle and an ash, willow, oak, or holly beater. Before flailing, the sheaf would be struck three times against a wooden block *(sou-*

Below: **Winnowing by hand. China.**

macher). There are other types of flails—in some Nepalese villages, for example, the beater consists of several wands tied together.

Winnowing

The wheat grains broken away from their clusters must be gathered and separated from their husks and impurities. In France this was done by means of a sieve or a shovel, and in Mediterranean countries by using a large, flat, two-handled willow basket, filled with the mixture to be winnowed and shaken so that the straw is carried away on the wind. From Turkey to Afghanistan, the method of choice is to toss the grain up, against the wind, using a wooden pitchfork, and letting it fall back at the worker's feet. The separation is later completed by sieving.

The Chinese devised a more sophisticated machine, the *tarare,* equipped with little flaps activated by a crank, to generate air movement. This air current blows away the straw and the grain falls into a drawer that is simply opened afterwards. The *tarare* reached parts of Europe, including France, Spain, and Turkey in the nineteenth century without any change in design—which bears witness to the excellence of its construction.

Right: **Winnowing by hand. India.**

I believe few people have thought much upon the strange multitude of little things necessary in the providing, producing, curing, dressing, making, and finishing this one article of bread.

I, that was reduced to a mere state of nature, found this to my daily discouragement; and was made more sensible of it every hour, even after I had got the first handful of seed-corn, which, as I have said, came up unexpectedly, and indeed to a surprise.

(Daniel Defoe, *Robinson Crusoe,*
The Project Gutenberg Etext)

Right: **Leon-Augustin Lhermitte**, *Paying the Harvesters*, 1882. Paris, Musée d'Orsay.

THE SAGA OF THE MILL

The grain is now ready to be milled. The seed itself is still protected by its coats: the pericarp, the hard shell which will be ground with the grain to form bran, separated in turn from the flour by sifting or bolting, and under this shell, the fine membrane of the protein layer, which contains the grain's kernel, and the germ. A wheat berry consists of about 14 to 16% non-digestible coatings, 81 to 83% kernel (grains of starch connected by gluten), and 2.5 to 3% germ. It measures about 6 mm and one thousand grains weigh about 45 grams.

Before milling was adopted, the age-old practice had been to crush the grain. In Neolithic times, it was crushed between a flat stone and a cylindrical one. In ancient Egypt, it was crushed first in a mortar and pestle, then on a large flat or slightly concave stone using the same roller. The Greeks used this method, as did the Romans, and it is still practiced in several Asian countries, as well as Yemen, to break down millet. The same stones also crush corn kernels in Mexico.

Below: **Traditional stone windmill near Santa Maria del Cami, Spain.**

The Handmill

The advent of the hand-operated mill simplified and rationalized the work, although it may not have lightened it. This mill consists of a stationary or "sleeper" stone and a moving one set on the first, centered on a pivot, and rotated using a handle or lever. Friction between the two grindstones crushes the grain and the flour runs out at the sides. For better efficiency, the upper surface of the stationary stone is scored.

Rotating millstones of this type have been found in Palestine, dating back to the second millennium B.C. They were known in Egypt—the Bible mentions a servant girl turning the mill for the Pharaoh *(Exodus, XI, 5),* and Homer's *Odyssey* recounts the complaint of the twelve servant women laboring to prepare a meal by crushing barley and wheat for Penelope's suitors. These mills appear on terra-cotta reliefs that date from the ninth century B.C. and which, according to Pliny, were brought to Italy by the Etruscans. In Rome, the mills are first mentioned by Marcus Porcius Cato (234–149 B.C.) in his *Re Rustica.*

These handmills, slow and hard to handle, were introduced to Northern Europe by the Celts before reaching England in the first century B.C. and they were used in France in Gallo-Roman times. But in the Middle Ages, with feudal privilege prevailing, French peasants were often not even allowed to own a simple handmill: they had to grind their grain at the theoretically "communal" mill which, in fact, belonged to the feudal lord. A variation on this mill, featuring an adjustable gap between the stones—to set the degree of grinding—was known in medieval England *(pot quern),* and still exists in Iran.

The Romans greatly improved the stone mill with a conical stationary stone and a tightly fitting rotating hollow stone. Such mills can still be found in Morocco: the wheat is poured into the upper flared section of the moving stone which acts as a hopper; the grain then gradually falls through four or five openings at the bottom of the funnel, and the seed lodged between these two stones is crushed and turned into flour, which flows out at the edges of the grindstone.

The volcanic eruption that engulfed Pompeii in A.D. 79 preserved some of its bakeries, in which several nearly intact mills, about two meters high, are lined up in the same room as the oven. Each mill was turned by two slaves circling around the grindstone; bas-reliefs at the Vatican Museum also show similar mills, with two horses instead of two slaves. These animals could also be harnessed to oil mills, as they still are in North Africa and the Near East. In Flanders, many such horse-driven mills, known as "carousel mills" or "trunnion mills," could still be found in the early 1950s, substituting for windmills when there was no wind.

Rome's belated adoption of circular and flat grindstones paved the way for water-driven upper stones in watermills, thus eliminating the need for slaves to turn a conical stone.

Above: **Stone handmill consisting of a stationary flat millstone, and of a moving millstone centered on a wooden pin and turned with a handle.**

Above: **To reach this flour mill in Corbeil-Essones, the wheat had to be transported in bulk on barges.**

Opposite: **Don Quixote and his faithful Sancho Panza in Arthur Hiller's film, *Man of La Mancha*, 1971.**

Pages 86–87: **The famous mills of La Mancha, in Spain, immortalized by Cervantes.**

The Watermill

A mill with a horizontal wheel and vertical shaft, driven both by the weight of the water and the force of the current which moves the grindstone directly without any transmission, was first mentioned by Strabo in connection with the palace of King Mithridates in 65 B.C. This type of mill was known in China as early as in the third or fourth century B.C., having been brought by the Persians or by the Greeks from Bactria. It was in use in the South of France during the nineteenth century, and can be found today in the mountains of Iran.

A second, more widespread, type of hydraulic mill requires a gear mechanism, a horizontal sys-tem for transmitting motion from the water-driven wheel to the vertical shaft that turns the moving grindstone. Vitruvius, chronicler of Roman tech-nology, first described this mechanism in his *De Architectura,* published between 20 and 11 B.C. Introduced by the Romans throughout the Em-pire, mills such as these met with extraordinary success. Their presence is recorded in Athens, Byzantium, all of fourth-century Gaul, and as far away as India. Eventually, they reached Germany and all of Central Europe. Vauban counted about 80,000 of them at the end of the seventeenth cen-tury (until the early nineteenth century, each mill could drive only one grindstone).

A third type, the floating vane-mill, was in-vented by the Romans while besieged by the Goths in A.D. 537. These mills, common in Mesopotamia and Iran in the tenth century, were also found eve-rywhere along French rivers, including several on the Seine in Paris, as early as the thirteenth cen-tury. Secured by a cable to a piling driven into the riverbed, they would be made fast to anchor onto bridge pillars—particularly at the Pont aux Meuniers or Millers' Bridge, downstream from the Pont au Change, so that they could take advantage of the acceleration of the current when the water levels dropped. Old postcards illustrating these floating mills can still be found.

The Windmill

The first windmills, which originated in Persia, had a vertical shaft that drove the upper grindstone directly without any transmission sys-tem. The writer Al-Mas'ûdî tells of a Persian slave boasting to the Caliph Oman (634–644) that he could build a windmill "which would be the talk of the world." The Persian writer places these fa-mous mills—in 956—east of Iran, in Seistan, a desert region where "the 120-day wind" blows in the spring. By the eleventh century, such mills had reached the islands of the Aegean Sea, Spain, and Portugal, with a shaft now leaning by 30% toward the horizontal. Vertical shaft mills still ex-ist in Seistan, in Khorassan, and in Iran, lined up at the edge of villages, although their numbers have tended to dwindle with the competition from

Diesel engines. They can also be found, however, in neighboring Afghanistan, around Herat, and in the Afghan Seistan.

A very different type of windmill made its way in Europe: it has a horizontal (or near horizontal) shaft, vertical arms, and a motion transmission system. Western writers disavow any oriental origin for this design. Yet, if the transmission system conceived by Romans for the very widely known hydraulic mill were simply added to the Iranian windmill, the result would be the European windmill. But, in fact, it only appeared in Europe in the twelfth century, after the Crusades (Jerusalem was conquered during the first Crusade in 1099), and mainly in Northern France where winds are very

predictable, as well as in England, Belgium, Holland, and Denmark. The first German mill of this type was built in 1393, and they became quite common in Europe in the fifteenth century.

The oldest windmill model is the "tower mill," a brick or stone building that has a permanent foundation set directly in the ground, and four to eight arms. With this design, frequently found on the outskirts of towns in Southern France and later in the North, the whips can only catch the wind head-on, so that the mill's roof must pivot to reorient them when the wind changes direction.

In the "pivoting mill," invented in Holland, the whole structure consists of a wooden frame which rests on a central pivot on the ground and which can turn with the wind. The design already appeared in thirteenth-century manuscript illustrations and it was successfully adopted in Flanders, Germany, and Northern France, where stone is scarce.

The Fate of Master Cornille

In medieval times, the mill belonged to the lord who retained exclusive rights to mill his subjects' wheat in exchange for a fee. This monopoly provoked numerous peasant revolts in Germany, England, and France. Elimination of the mills' so-called "communality" was to be one of the grievances presented in 1789, and the laws of March 15–28, 1790, abolished this lordly privilege along with the "communal" rights over bread-baking ovens.

Still, time was running out for windmills, as well as for small-scale millers. Less than a century later, in "Le Secret de Maître Cornille," one of the tales from his *Lettres de mon moulin* (*Letters from My Windmill,* 1866), Alphonse Daudet wrote of the merciless competition from the steam-driven industrial mills which were responsible for the disappearance of windmills.

Since the 1930s, a preservation movement sponsored by several associations has been working to save the windmills which have been decimated by the industrial revolution and the Diesel engine. Many mills are being purchased and restored throughout Europe, and the whips of these age-old

At this point they came in sight of thirty or forty windmills that are on that plain, and as soon as Don Quixote saw them he said to his squire, "Fortune is arranging matters for us better than we could have shaped our desires ourselves, for look there, friend Sancho Panza, where thirty or more monstrous giants present themselves, all of whom I mean to engage in battle and slay, and with whose spoils we shall begin to make our fortunes; for this is righteous warfare, and it is God's good service to sweep so evil a breed from off the face of the earth."

"What giants?" said Sancho Panza.

"Those thou seest there," answered his master, "with the long arms, and some have them nearly two leagues long."

"Look, your worship," said Sancho; "what we see there are not giants but windmills, and what seem to be their arms are the sails that turned by the wind make the millstone go."

(Cervantes, *Don Quixote*, Chapter VIII,
The Project Gutenberg Etext, translated by John Ormsby)

Above: **One of the last traditional windmills in France, tower-shaped, with vertical arms and a motion transmission system. The millstone is on the lower level (Moulin de Chesnay in Moutiers, Beauce).**

mills have resumed turning, exposing their beautiful mechanisms to wonder-struck visitors: there are about ten of these mills in Belgium and Holland, and several hundred in Portugal; France still has a few in the Vendée, in Eure-et-Loir, and in Coquelles near Calais. At Ivry, outside Paris, people can visit the Moulin de la Tour, which is the last one left in Val-de-Marne, while Maine-et-Loire boasts six mills registered as historic monuments.

Countless other old mills have become secondary residences, hotels, or, occasionally, museums. The French Federation of the Friends of the Mills has inventoried 10,000 watermills and 3,000 windmills. Some of these, like the Moulin de Boisse at Castelnau-Montratier in the Lot region, operate only on August 15 during harvest festivals.

The Modern Milling Plant

After centuries of coarse, poorly sifted bread, many people dreamed of white wheat bread, once the bread of the rich. Soon after 1830, this dream was to become reality, thanks to the invention of a Swiss engineer by the name of Müller, who designed a mill with steam-driven metal rollers that could produce a whiter flour. This machine, improved by Jacob Sulzberger for the Swiss market, was first purchased by Hungary, then by Americans from Minnesota, who brought Hungarian engineers over to the United States in 1879, after the Vienna Universal Exposition of 1873. The modern flour mill era was about to begin.

Nowadays, flour mills are almost entirely automated. The wheat moves through a series of sorters, washers, dampeners, dryers, and brushes, before being ground progressively finer through four reduction stages called grinding, sifting, clapping, and conversion.

Types of Flour

Grades of flour are classified according to their extraction ratio, i.e. the weight of flour (purified of waste by sifting) obtained per one hundred kilograms of milled wheat. For example, a yield of 75 kg of flour from 100 kg of wheat is called a 75% sifted flour, or a flour with a 75% extraction ratio. This flour, marketed under the name of "type 55," is the one most commonly used by bakeries for white bread. But the mills offer a wide selection, ranging from whole wheat flour (type 150), which contains the complete berry, to the whitest flour (type 45), sifted dozens of times, and used for Danish and fine pastries.

Fiber, protein, vitamin, and mineral content is reduced as sifting is increased to produce a whiter flour. With the increasing popularity of "old-fashioned" breads, the new types of flour are designed to retain nutritional elements, and whiteness is no longer such an absolute requirement. The flour used for bran bread is only sifted to 85–90%, for whole wheat to 90–95%, and to 98% for whole-grain bread. Artisan bakers, who knead, shape, and bake their own breads, have their own special requirements, depending on the ovens they use and the bread they produce.

Today's mills produce a great variety of quality flours formulated for modern tastes, which may range from whole wheat, mixed grain, bran, organic, and stone-ground, to newly rediscovered flours, such as spelt.

Master Cornille was an old miller who had lived for sixty years amid flour and was enraged by his circumstances. The advent of industrial mills had driven him nearly mad. For eight days, he was seen running about the village, gathering everybody around him and shouting at the top of his lungs about a plot to poison Provence with industrial flour. "Don't go there," he kept saying. "Those thugs are making bread with steam, which is an invention of the devil, whereas I work with the winds of the Mistral and Tramontane, which are the breath of the Good Lord. . . ." And on he went, heaping praise upon windmills but finding that no one would listen to him.

Whereupon, out of sheer rage, the old man locked himself up in his mill and lived there all alone like a wild beast.

(Alphonse Daudet, *Lettres de mon moulin,* "Le Secret de Maître Cornille"
Letters from My Windmill: "The Secret of Master Cornille")

Right: **Some examples of flour used by contemporary bakers.**

The *Petit Journal* Campaign

On October 26, 1895, the periodical *Le Petit Journal* launched a vehement campaign entitled "Return to the Grindstone" in favor of bran bread made with stone-ground flour as opposed to white bread from roller-milled flour. The issue had been raised originally by a well-known professor at the Faculté de Paris, Professor Tournier, who had pointed out the dangers of white bread, suspected of causing dyspeptic disturbances, convulsions, and other problems of the nervous system in children. The issue at stake in this debate was clear: a condemnation of the roller method and a return to millstone bread.

These disclosures caused quite a stir in public opinion, as well as in the profession: within a few days, over five hundred bakers came to the newspaper's offices on Rue Lafayette to join the movement, promising to deliver the vaunted new bread. But after several weeks of such a diet, Parisians began to have second thoughts. According to M. Barlich, a campaign spokesman, "the flour mills, recently organized to produce the grade of flour known as 'fine white flour,' had managed to turn Parisians forever against organic bread, in other words bread sifted at 85%." And by what means! By invoking the new bread as a pretext to use spoiled flour, or products that had not been stripped of the coarse bran; and even by introducing paper, shredded straw, wood shavings, and other foreign bodies into the bread—or so rumor had it. Under these conditions, the "new" bread could only be mediocre and difficult to digest. In short, organic bread was a failure and white bread triumphed.

A similar campaign in favor of "standard bread" was launched a few years later in England. As in France, it started with a number of scientific studies pointing to the harmful effects of white bread on health. This campaign had an even greater impact—all families, all social classes, the English aristocracy, and even the king himself, adopted standard bread. Everyone wanted to eat it. Some six thousand bakers agreed to make this miracle bread, whose success seemed guaranteed. Alas! One year later, nothing was left of it save "an odiously tainted bread," according to one commentator.

Falsification? Sabotage? Manipulation? Nothing about these two campaigns is very clear. Voices were raised against the flour mills, denouncing their suspicious activities. But the harm had been done. Thus discredited, stone-ground bread was to relinquish supremacy to white bread for nearly a century.

LE LIVRE POPULAIRE

XAVIER DE MONTÉPIN

LA PORTEUSE DE PAIN

LE VOLUME COMPLET

65 CENTIMES

A. FAYARD ÉDITEUR PARIS

Le Petit Journal

ADMINISTRATION 61, RUE LAFAYETTE, 61	**15** CENT.	SUPPLÉMENT ILLUSTRÉ	**15** CENT.	ABONNEMENTS

Les manuscrits ne sont pas rendus — 31me Année — Numéro 1.524.

On s'abonne sans frais dans tous les bureaux de poste

DIMANCHE 7 MARS 1920

	SIX MOIS	UN AN
France et Colonies.....	5 fr.	8 fr.
Etranger	6 fr.	10 fr.

LE PAIN
Tout le monde, aujourd'hui, mange du pain blanc.
NE LE GASPILLONS PAS !

The End of the Bread Eaters?

In the days when bread was bread, people knew what it meant to "earn your bread by the sweat of your brow," as the late-nineteenth-century *Livreurs de farine (The Flour Deliverymen)* attests. But even the most immutable things come to an end. Everything changed between the two World Wars. The man of the people, Western man, the inveterate eater of bread, the bread for which he had fought a revolution, became slowly but surely a meat eater. Timidly at first, then with greater voracity. Such was the mark of progress, the symbol of a better life. It was a new revolution, apparent on dinner plates but also in the language: it was no longer "earn your bread" but "bring home the bacon." Bread had lost its first battle. Could it be that the retreat of Neolithic man, born with the advent of grain cultivation some eight thousand years before the Christian era, heralded a return to Paleolithic man, the big game hunter? Still, there is evidence that the bread eaters have not had their final say.

Left: **Louis Robert Carrier-Belleuse,**
The Flour Deliverymen, 1885.
Paris, Musée du Petit-Palais.

BREAD-BAKING OVENS

Were the Egyptians the first to introduce the notion of oven baking? Several Egyptian paintings show molds being filled with dough, sealed, and set to bake over a fire. The breads discovered in Egyptian tombs, hermetically sealed in bowls and buried for the deceased's journey to the next world, were probably baked in this way.

Embers and Ashes

In North Africa, some leavened breads are cooked in a covered clay platter placed on embers. This platter can also be found in Provence, where it is called *diable-rousset* and consists of two pink terra-cotta skillets fitted together that are buried under the ashes to cook the bread. In ancient Greece, *cribanite* was cooked in a dish covered with a lid perforated to admit heat, and placed amid the glowing embers. In ancient Rome, a sort of whole wheat household bread or *authophirus* was baked in a *cacabus,* which was probably a covered clay receptacle. A similar method existed in Yugoslavia during the Bronze Age, and still survives in Romania.

In parts of Ireland, at least as recently as the middle of the twentieth century, bread was baked in a corner of the hearth in a cast iron kettle whose lid was covered with embers. This technique was also used by French Canadian lumberjacks to make *pains de chantier* (camp bread) in a covered cast-iron cauldron containing the dough and buried under wood embers, and by Canadian peasants for *fesses de pain* (bread "buns") cooked in pairs in a pot. Many a soldier, issued flour instead of bread, has become familiar with the *pain de marmite,* or kettle bread, which used to be cooked in a metal receptacle and would come out in the shape of the pot. French housewives also baked their bread that way during the last war. I have also seen it made this way—unleavened—in Afghanistan by the semi-nomadic Uzbeks for whom the method was a relic of the days when their nomadic ancestors had no ovens. Such breads can weigh as much as 7 kilos; when time is short, they are prepared in the morning for the meal that will be served to the family, guests, and workers.

Left: **Communal oven.**

Encamped Roman soldiers roasted their *panis militaris* or *panis subcinerarius* under the ashes, in the open air, as did the Greeks with their *eucryphies*. And any wanderer, pilgrim, merchant, or other traveler throughout Central Asia in the nineteenth century knew this technique. It was also familiar to Arminius Vambery, the great Hungarian explorer who, in 1864, disguised as a mystical dervish, reached the holy, forbidden city of Bukhara: "For my part, I could see my flour supply dwindling so fast that I felt obliged from then on to limit myself to a survival portion and cut back my daily ration by two handfuls. I was also careful not to leaven my bread before cooking it under the ashes: the result is more substantial, it does not travel as fast through the digestive tract, and hunger pangs are fewer and far between."[4] This method has not disappeared. The Bible mentions flatbread cooked in camel dung embers. I have eaten this bread, and believe me, it was really very good. I was walking in Afghanistan with a small group of men, traveling to Faizabad three days away, one of whom was reporting for military service, a second on his way to market to buy fabric, tea, and matches for the winter (cheaper than at any store), while the third planned to trade some dried fruit. We were getting hungry and so we stopped to eat. One of my companions took a few handfuls of flour from a little cloth bag and, adding a little bit of the water he had brought, began to knead it in a wooden bowl. Another walked off to collect the abundant dromedary dung dropped by the herds which had pastured there that summer (it was now September). Once the fire had been lit, we had to wait for the embers to build up. One of the men then used his walking stick to spread them out, and placed the disks of dough, a few centimeters thick, atop the bed of hot ashes. When the embers were piled up to cover the dough, they became an oven within which the bread could bake. About fifteen minutes later, when the embers were cleared out of the way with the stick, you could see the cooked flatbread. All you had to do was blow away the ashes and pick out the bits of coal stuck to it. My companions hunkered down, and invited me to join them.

Above: **Baking flat cakes in the warm Sahara sands of Southern Tunisia.**

Pages 96–97: **Bread oven. Cairo, Egypt.**

The Oriental Oven

Before any ovens were built, they were improvised using hot earth: here again, the French Canadian woodsmen would place their bread dough in a sandy patch heated with a big fire. The buried bread would take one hour and a half to bake. In Iceland, bread is still cooked this way. Buried in spots naturally heated by volcanic activity, the dough remains in the ground for thirty hours.

Nomads in the north and northwest of Iran would heat up a hole in the ground, and once the sides were hot enough, they would remove the ashes and deposit the dough at the bottom. The hole was then covered with a plate or a metal sheet that was topped with embers, and the flatbread would cook in this oven (the *tâbûn*). The nomads of Khorasan and Baluchistan add an aerated hole dug into the ground and they slap the flat cakes against the oven's sides.

The first real oven, made of hardened mud, was shaped like a truncated cone. Set on the ground, it is open at the top, with an air intake hole at the base. A brush fire is lighted at the bottom. Once the sides are hot enough, the flames are extinguished with water while the accumulated embers retain the heat. The various breads, flat and circular, are slapped against the inner walls of the oven very quickly because the hand and arm have to go through the opening at the top. Then, once the bread is baked and before it can fall down into the oven, it is taken out, usually with an iron spike.

This type of oven is extremely ancient. It can be found in a somewhat more cylindrical version in buried Egyptian paintings such as those on the tomb of Ramses III, together with representations of the convex plates used to cook flatbread, and the skillets used to fry dough.

Opposite: **The rural oven of the Orient is a cone-shaped mud and wattle structure. Women place the flatbreads by hand on the oven griddles, which are heated with brushwood gathered on the steppes.**

Pages 100–101: **Baking hard-wheat bread in a village oven in Morocco.**

Below: **The Near-Eastern traditional bakery oven, set below ground: two workers shape the dough into long flatbreads, while a third loads the oven and uses two iron spears to remove the breads cooked inside on the oven walls. Afghanistan.**

This Egyptian oven was probably suitable for cooking the flat, lightly leavened bread disks, dotted at the center with a bread stamp, that have been unearthed from Eighteenth Dynasty tombs (c. 1400 B.C.).

This type of oven, sixty to eighty centimeters high, is well adapted to poorly wooded regions because it works very well with desert brush, and has always been the one used by the sedentary peasants of the Near East. It is found among all the populations of Central Asia, in India, the Caucasus, Syria, Lebanon, Turkey, Tunisia, Yemen, and Egypt to this day.

Among Iranians, who make an elongated bread that is larger and more delicate, the oven *(tanûr)* is set into an earthen shelf or buried. The lightly leavened bread is usually made of wheat (but barley, millet, or corn may also be used). The yeast added to the dough is prepared from a bit of day-old dough that has been diluted in hot water. The dough may be stamped with a wooden seal that leaves a design in relief. Iranians still make "stone bread" or *nân-e sangak,* which is cooked on a bed of smooth stones heated at the bottom of a bread oven, with a few hot stones set on top to accelerate the baking.

The European Oven

The Oriental oven's truncated cone, meant only for flatbreads, was hardly suitable for collective baking in "communal" ovens, or for the intensive production of Western bakers.

The European oven is a closed model, consisting of a dome-shaped vault above a horizontal surface or floor, upon which the breads are placed after the embers which have heated the oven have been swept away.

The simplest design, a baked clay hemisphere wide open at the front but with no other vent for the smoke, dates back to the days of the Roman Republic. It was also shown later in woodcuts from Germany (in 1350) and from Strasbourg (in 1502).

In Spain, several Castilian villages still specialize in producing these baked clay ovens, hand-crafted by women potters. They are sold

Below: **Illustration of a European oven in Kharga, Egypt. Arabic characters spell "Welcome" and "God's Blessings on Your Behalf Are Infinite."**

Above: **European horizontal oven closed with an iron door. Karpathos Island, Greece.**

throughout the entire region, where women still bake their own bread once a week. This oven, which can hold up to six loaves, is integrated into an earthen structure for better heat retention. During the baking process, its opening is blocked by an iron plate. Such ovens must be rebuilt from time to time, since they eventually crack from the heat. In the Balkans and in Hungary, this oven is raised and surrounded by a thickness of earth, and set outside the house under a canopy.

The Pompeii Model

The most widely used oven in the European countryside was inspired by the famous Pompeii oven: it features a stone or brick vault set over a flat floor, instead of the baked clay cupola that is fragile and whose capacity is too limited. These very sturdy ovens are sometimes very large and can serve the needs of an entire village. They exist wherever country people have retained the custom of making their own bread about once a week—not only in France, but throughout Europe as far distant as Sardinia and Greece. (The Roman-style oven has even migrated to farms in Canada and the United States.)

The design for this oven provides for only one opening, used to load the fire logs and to remove the embers with a small scraper once the oven is hot, and where the bread is inserted. Such an oven is often located outside the house because the wood smoke escapes through the same opening during the heating stage and creates a fire hazard. In some improved models installed inside living areas, the smoke is collected and vented through a hood in front of the oven.

The stone floor (granite in the Cévennes) is known to sometimes burn the bread set on it. The introduction of refractory bricks corrects this problem, perfecting the oven's design and solidity. The opening is sometimes equipped with a thick metal plate to prevent heat loss.

This oven, known as a *direct intermittent heat oven* (because the flames come into direct contact with the surface that will hold the bread and the embers are removed once it is hot enough), is sometimes replaced by a more elaborate type whose great advantage is that it does not need to be emptied or cleaned before each load. In this *indirect intermittent heating* oven, the fuel is placed in a hearth under the floor that is connected to the oven through an opening called the "throat," equipped with a moveable device which allows the baker to direct the flames toward various areas of the oven.

This technique was introduced very early in France, since it was mentioned in a late fourteenth-century manuscript at the Bibliothèque Nationale, then appeared in many woodcuts beginning in the fifteenth century, and could later be seen in engravings of the Rembrandt School. By the eighteenth century, when all bakers had adopted it, the oven was built of refractory bricks and with double doors, which—by the end of the nineteenth century—had become a single, counterweighted vertical sliding door. This woodburning system, just like the grindstone, is still to be found today in some bakeries—as a result of the current vogue for "old-fashioned" bread.

Left: **Industrial bakery in
the United States.**

The Contemporary Oven

Whether electric, oil, or gas fired, equipped with pulsed air or steam, modern ovens provide a continuous heat, which is more suitable for certain kinds of delicate-crust breads such as the baguette. These ovens include an automatic misting device that operates during the baking cycle, producing the beautiful golden color that customers demand. Not so long ago, bakers still had to insert a wet straw plug into the oven just before loading (a procedure also familiar to housewives), a nearly universal practice used to humidify the oven, or they had to sprinkle water on the loaves once they were in place. Otherwise, the bread would remain gray.

Ovens are becoming more automated every year: continuous heat, fixed floor ovens with heat circulation conduits around multiple baking chambers; continuous heat, moveable floor ovens; as well as rack ovens and tunnel ovens for industrial applications. Not to mention tests in microwave ovens that may some day bake our baguettes in the blink of an eye (rather than in the 20 minutes at 250°C required today).

THE BREAD OF NOMADS

In the beginning there was a cereal gruel, such as *bulgur,* a preparation of boiled crushed wheat still frequently found in the Turkish countryside. Then came a flatbread, cooked on hot stones, made first from grain crushed on a stone, and later from ground flour.

This flatbread used an unleavened dough. It was the original bread, the bread of nomads, of unfettered men. Far removed from the bread made of flaky or non-flaky dough as defined in our dictionaries, this wheat or corn bread has always been the mainstay of hundreds of millions of people in America, North Africa, the Near East, and India. In those countries, in fact, the same word has been used to designate all breads, whether leavened or not.

"Bread on a Metal Sheet"

The nomads of the Near and Middle East cannot burden themselves with a bread oven. As a result, they eat an unleavened, thin, circular bread made of wheat flour and cooked on a flat or slightly convex iron plate. The plate is heated over a fire, and when it reaches the right temperature, the women place on it a sheet of dough which they have flattened and shaped evenly between their palms. The dough is thin, cooks very rapidly, and does not need to be turned.

The same gestures, the same technique have endured for over three thousand years. Egyptian tomb paintings depict this fine, circular bread being cooked on a convex metal plate.

In Anatolian villages, the bread cooked on a metal sheet is called *sipit,* and the wood that will be burned under it is chosen as carefully as possible so that it may impart its fragrance to the bread. The *yüfka* or sheet of dough used to make stuffed bread, or *börek,* is even thinner: once cooked, it is kept covered for a few days, then moistened before assembling the *börek.* A similar sheet of cooked, brittle dough is used in North Africa to prepare pasties or fritters, and is sold in Arab or Jewish shops in France for the preparation of egg and vegetable fritters.

The Turkish sheets of dough used for the honey-flavored pastry called *baklava,* are finer still. On the other hand, in the poor villages where not so long ago bread was only cooked every twenty days at most, the sheets are thicker and must be turned over on the metal plate to cook both sides. Before the meal, they are moistened and rolled up in a cloth to soften. Some of these unleavened flatbreads (*sipit*) are made of corn flour (*misir ekme*) or oats (*arpa ekme*). The Yörük nomads make a similar cake of millet flour: the *dari ekme.* Still another Turkish specialty is long, unleavened flatbread eaten at the evening meal during the fasting period of Ramadan.

The *nân-e sâj,* the "metal sheet bread," or *nàn-e fatîrî* of Iran is prepared in nomad encampments from unleavened dough (*khamîr*) cooked on a metal plate for two or three minutes. Sometimes, in order to enhance its flavor, poppy seeds or *asafoetida,* extracted from a desert plant, are added just before the bread is cooked. The Pachounes of Afghanistan also use an iron griddle, and many nomads retain the custom once they become sedentary, because it makes very fine and delicious bread. The people of Pakistan and India use the same method to cook *chapati,* the peasant bread that is served with various legumes. Morning and evening, Indian villages echo with the sound of women slapping the sheets of dough between their palms to make them even thinner. This dough is composed of wheat flour and water, kneaded, shaped into balls, and left to rest for a half hour.

The Carta da Musica

Italy has kept the old tradition of the *piada,* an unleavened bread cooked on the hearth on a tripod with a flat metal surface. This bread contains only flour and water, and being fairly thick, must be turned over on the griddle. It is still eaten frequently in the Romagna countryside, where it is considered the regional bread, just like the very fine flatbread called *carta da musica* or "sheet music" in Sardinia.

Opposite: **Among the nomads of Jordan, thin unleavened dough flatbreads are baked on an iron griddle heated with embers.**

In France, crêpes used to be the staple of the traditional diet in Brittany. These buckwheat ("black wheat") crêpes cooked on a metal griddle, usually with salt and sometimes with other garnishes, were originally the true Breton bread before becoming the cake or dessert we think of today. Farmers used to make them for their workers during periods of intensive fieldwork. The poor ate virtually nothing else, and they were widely served with cod as abstinence meals on the fast days of Tuesdays and Fridays. Crêpes can also be eaten in soup, shredded into whey or churned milk, as they do in Saint-Malo. Crêpes drizzled with olive oil and garnished with a slice of meat and an onion are a Celtic tradition.

Firestones

Among the non-Islamic Kalash, the iron griddle *(hunza)*—which would have to be purchased—is replaced in poor households by a large stone slab, which costs nothing and doubtless represents a much older tradition. Similarly, in Southern Afghanistan, nomads on the move carry with them a large flat stone for cooking their flatbread.

The lumberjacks in their vast Northern Canadian camps did not burden themselves with stones. They could cook their bread on a boulder, upon which they would build a great fire with the wood so plentifully available. Then they would push the ashes aside, set the dough on the hot rock, and add a few embers on top to accelerate the baking.

Tajine and Tanûr

One of the ancient Roman breads, *artopticius,* was a fine flour flatbread cooked in a pan or a skillet. In North Africa, unleavened flatbread coexists with leavened bread baked in the oven. In

Left: **A Kirghiz woman bakes her bread inside a yurt. Afghanistan.**

wheats, watered only by the spring rains, are preferred to irrigated crops grown in the valleys,
where yield is increased at the expense of flavor.
For festivals, the bread is enhanced with milk,
eggs, butter, sugar, or even whey. The surfaces of
these loaves are more elaborately decorated,
using antique bronze seals or imprinting them
with a key design stamped all around the edge.

In Yemen, circles of dough leavened with
starter yeast are slapped against the oven's inner
walls, where they cook in barely a minute. These
breads, called *jehein,* are made of sorghum flour.
An unleavened version is reserved for the ritual
evening meal during the period of fasting—it is
the *lelueh,* a thin flatbread cooked on a metal
griddle set on the top opening of the oven, then
shredded into sour milk.

The large, very thin and flat *lavash* of the
Iranians and the Armenians is also unleavened or
almost so—once cooked, it is "almost as thin
as paper." It can also be prepared by urban bakers
who have kept the traditional oven *(tanur)* and
even improved upon it.

Although the function of the baker is to
produce leavened bread (isn't that why we go
there, to buy the bread that we don't have time to
bake ourselves?), it is apparent from the examples
in Iran and Central Asia that the line between
leavened and unleavened bread, between yeast
and no yeast, is not as distinct as it might seem at
first. The same breads can be sometimes leavened, sometimes not, depending upon the region.
And the difference is often minimal between an
unleavened bread which has been left to rest and,
therefore, has started to ferment, and a bread to
which a bit of water mixed with leavening from
the previous day's dough has been added, but
which has not been given time to rise.

Right: **Preparing *lavash*, the
thin crisp flatbread of Iran
and Armenia.**

THE TORTILLA: BREAD OF MEXICO

One of the most frequently used words in daily conversation in Mexico is *tortilla* (omelet, in Spanish), for the corn flat cake that comprises the basic diet of the entire peasant population, as well as of many city dwellers. The *tortilla* is the basic bread of Mexicans; it shows up at all meals, and among the least affluent it may amount to virtually the entire meal.

As recently as twenty or thirty years ago, throughout the countryside, *tortillas* were made in the same way and with the same utensils as in the sixteenth century, at the time of the Spanish Conquest. Two implements are indispensable for making *tortillas:* the grindstone and the *comal.* The grindstone consists of the *metate* together with its "hand." The *metate* is a rectangular volcanic flat stone, leaning forward on three or four legs; its *mano,* or hand, is a cylindrical roller made of the same kind of material which is rubbed against the flat stone. The *comal* is a circular, unglazed, slightly concave fired clay plate.

Women's Work

Making the *tortillas* is exclusively women's work. The women boil the corn kernels for several hours in an earthenware pot, in water containing lime. This boiled corn, called *nixtamal,* is carefully rinsed in clear water. In some regions, the women set their grindstone on a table and work standing up; others kneel down and set it on the ground. They grind the boiled corn kernels for a long time with the *mano* against the *metate,* adding water as needed. This produces a dough, the *masa,* which becomes finer the longer the corn is ground. A wood fire is then lit among three stones, and the griddle is placed on top. The cook takes a little ball of dough which she flattens between her hands to form a flat cake, which she then sets directly on the *comal* without using any fat.

This work is long and tiring. The mother must rise before dawn to prepare the breakfast *tortillas,* and early in the afternoon she starts making more for the evening meal. Each preparation takes three hours, but in the city, the *tortillas* are

machine-made. However, everyone agrees that the handmade ones are far more delicious; that is why even city women often make their own, buying *maseca,* the dehydrated dough which becomes *masa* with the addition of water. The flat cake is shaped from a little ball of dough flattened in a mold: the principle is the same, and the work is reduced to a minimum.

Made by hand or by machine, the *tortilla* has always maintained its importance in the diet of most Mexicans, and plays a far greater role in their meals than bread does in today's European countries. Very often, peasants eat meat just once or twice a week, or only on holidays, while their

Below: **Growing corn and cooking *tortillas* on a round fired clay or metal griddle. Detail of a Diego Rivera fresco.**

diet consists essentially of black beans and chili peppers the rest of the time. The poorest among them, such as certain Mixtec Indians, eat nothing but *tortillas* with chili sauce.

In Mexico, townspeople adopted other forms of bread centuries ago, but corn *tortillas* show up at the best tables, across all social classes, whenever a typical Mexican dish is served. No one would even think of dispensing with the *tortillas* when enjoying a dish of *mole* (turkey in a brown chili sauce containing eighteen ingredients, including chocolate).

The *tortillas* are made a few hours before the meal and reheated as needed on the *comal* (or on the metal griddle that has replaced it today in many households), because they must be eaten hot. They are better when cooked at the last minute and that is how they are served to honored guests, meaning that someone has to be on duty before and during the entire meal. Even if they are prepared in advance, the custom is that a young girl or woman brings the hot ones to the table, takes away those that were not eaten immediately and so have cooled off, brings fresh hot ones, and so on until the end of the meal.

Different Table Manners

The Spaniards' astonishment at this "Mexican bread" is understandable: corn instead of wheat, a flatbread without yeast instead of leavened bread, a technique and some implements never seen before, the need to make the flat cakes every day, twice a day, and to serve them hot. Not only is the service different but so are the table manners, since table settings are no longer needed. The *tortilla* is torn into pieces held pincerwise between thumb and forefinger and used to scoop up a piece of meat; or the *tortilla* section can be shaped into a cone to pick up broth or sauces; as a result, the "fork" and "spoon" are swallowed with each bite without getting the fingers dirty. The *tortilla* or *masa* is basic to many other culinary specialties, each as flavorful as the next: *tacos, enchiladas, tostaditas, gorditas, chalupitas, chilaquiles, quesadillas.* Before roads were built, each journey on foot included a supply, not of *tortillas,*

which spoil rapidly, but of *totopoztli* — *tortillas* that have been grilled to a crisp.

Throughout central Mexico, a proper *tortilla* must be thin and light. In Mayan country, it is larger, thicker, and no longer central to the diet. Mayan peasants consume a great deal of *posole,* a nourishing liquid made of corn diluted with water, and often accompanied by tubers. To the North, at the other end of the country, the Tarahumara make *tortillas* only for holiday meals. Their daily diet consists of *izquiate,* grilled corn cooked in a broth with green vegetables.

Above: **Preparing *tortillas*.
Pre-Columbian fresco,
Teotihuacan, Mexico.**

HOMEMADE BREAD

This was the kind of bread that used to be made at home, on the farm, or in the communal village oven. Until the end of the nineteenth century, this household bread constituted the daily bread for the great majority of people. The decline of rural society, the proliferation of bakeries, as well as a reduction in bread consumption, have all contributed to its disappearance in the period between the two World Wars. What did this old-fashioned bread look like? It was usually a big round loaf weighing 5 to 6 kilos, like the oversize *tourtes* from the Auvergne or Savoy mountains, whose diameter could exceed "three or four feet." This was a heavy, nourishing kind of bread that would keep for several months.

In most regions, homemade bread consisted of mixed flours: rye stretched with barley, combinations of wheat and rye (called *méteil*), or of rye and buckwheat, like the bread familiar to agricultural workers in the Cévennes around the 1820s. It was very coarsely ground, with barely crushed kernel fragments and most of the bran left in the flour. This nutritious, vitamin-rich bread would be equivalent to what is today called "whole grain bread."

Baked infrequently—perhaps every two weeks in the summer and only once a month in winter, as on the Briançon farms—homemade bread mobilized the energy of everyone in the family or village. Only large farms had private ovens, while everyone else baked their bread in the village's communal oven.

The preparation of homemade bread is surrounded by elaborate rituals, know-how, and ancestral gestures. First the yeast, passed on from one household to the next so that there is always

Right: **Long ago, in the French countryside, the dough would be set to rise beneath the warm conjugal bed covers.**

Above: **Risen and shaped dough is brought to the village oven. Karpathos Island, Greece.**

Opposite: **Women bring dough for baking in the village oven. Dodecanese Islands, Greece.**

area for communal bread baking. Emilie Carles, in a story called *Une soupe aux herbes sauvages (A Soup of Wild Grasses)* explains: "the problem was to heat the oven to the right temperature. . . . Once it was hot, it was easy, you just had to maintain it, but whoever was first to bake his bread took the chance that the oven wouldn't be hot enough. This is why, once the bundles of wood were ready, in order to avoid disagreements and unfairness, the peasants drew lots. It was a regular lottery: everyone drew a number on a little piece of paper folded in a hat, and that was it [. . .]. The one who drew number one, drew the chore. He would be the one who had to light the oven and heat it. It was an extremely demanding job. For ten or more hours, one had to shovel in cords and cords of wood, without ever knowing if the oven temperature was right. After that though, it was a lot easier, since the oven was broken in." When the bread came out, it still had to be cooled before it could be stored on a rack or in the attic, on suspended trestles if it had to last the whole winter.

Was this homemade bread, this old-fashioned bread, good or not? It is not easy to form an opinion, since people's responses and recollections are so divergent. According to some, it was bad—badly ground, badly sieved of bran, badly cooked. Others have kept an idealized image of childhood bread, with surely a good dose of nostalgia among its ingredients.

One thing at least is certain: that bread was hard, hard and often stale. "In order to cut it," Emilie Carles goes on to say, "we had a special knife; it was so hard that it would shatter in pieces that landed all over the kitchen. But it was good . . . that bread had an extraordinary fragrance, and what a taste! My sisters and I would fight over it, we used to suck on it with delight as if it had been cake." The homemade bread of the 1900s in Gévaudan was just as good, "with its thick blackish crust, and so hard that the head of the house needed a well-honed knife to cut everybody's share. The inside, heavy and compact, very light brown, would mix with the saliva and become slightly sticky against the roof of the mouth as it was chewed."[6]

a fresh supply; then the kneading of the dough in a *maits à pétrir,* or mixing trough, a demanding task almost always done by women. "For the bread to be well made and flavorful," writes A. Goursaud, "the dough had to be pliable, homogeneous, fermenting (the word used was 'rising') very evenly. This kneading required a certain skill; that is why a recognition of the talent in a young girl of 'being good at making bread' was often sufficient grounds for agreement to a marriage which would not have occurred otherwise."[5]

Once the dough was shaped and set in the pans, the delicate and demanding watch over its fermentation would begin. In 1900, in the Limousin, the loaves would occasionally be slipped under the comforter to be kept warm when the weather turned very cold. Last came the oven, heated with bundles of dry wood or broom as the dough continued to rise in the *palisses,* and the embers were raked back to the mouth of the oven with a scraper. The job of heating the oven was usually entrusted to an experienced man, but sometimes other methods were used, such as in the Briançon

The tradition of homemade bread has not completely disappeared in France. In the Alps, various villages, such as Villar-d'Arêne, still organize collective bakings, but these communal customs now have a mainly commemorative value.

Except for such rare cases, the tradition of homemade bread was effectively diminished in the 1920s, by which time it was already on the wane. As a result, our imagination conjures up a golden age, a perhaps implausible time when bread would have been truly flavorful, thick-crusted, and with a sweet-smelling interior. But could it be that this exceptional bread of yesteryear is something of a myth?

He asked:
—What are you going to do?

(Nearly knowing the answer already, seeing the signs, but not daring to believe them, because it had become so new.)

And Madame Bertrand said:

—I'm going to make bread.

She set out the flour, Bertrand went to get water, and while he was at the fountain she understood that this bread was truly woman's work, work for which you need some maternity, so to speak, but for which you also need seduction. And she understood this joyfully, mischievously, deep within, clear as a bell, the way young girls understand love: and yet she, she is easily sixty-five.

Bertrand came back with the water buckets.

—Here you are!

—What do you mean, here you are, you silly man, what makes you think women do the kneading? The fat ones, maybe. The ones who look like men, maybe, but me?

And the fact is, she looks like a cricket.

—And so what?

—And so, she said, you have to take off your coat, and take off your shirt, and get down to it, you with your big arms.

(Jean Giono, *Les Vraies Richesses*)

Bread for a Lifetime

Homemade bread, as we know, was destined to last a long time. Mountain people in the Forez, Auvergne, or Savoy regions, in particular, baked enormous loaves that would keep for several months—sometimes even for a year. That is certainly a respectable age for any loaf of bread, and yet it pales in comparison to the longevity records achieved in some Northern countries: Valmont-Bomare relates that in Norway, they used to make a type of bread that could be kept for forty years! He writes: "It is a convenience, because once a man in those parts earns enough to get what he needs to make bread, he makes enough to last him all his life and thus will never need to fear famine." This bread, with such a long shelf life, is a sort of biscuit made with a flour composed of barley and oats, kneaded together, and cooked between two hollow stones. When it is fresh, it is almost tasteless; but the older it gets, the tastier it becomes, "so that," the author goes on to say, "people of this country are as fond of hard bread as others elsewhere are of soft bread. So it is not surprising that these people are careful to set some aside for celebrations to come—it is not unusual for bread that was made when a grandfather was born to be eaten on the occasion of the birth of his grandchild."

Left: **Country bread.**

RYE AND ITS TRADITIONS

Traditionally, rye has occupied the same place in the Northern and Central European diet that wheat has around the Mediterranean; this in spite of the fact that its competition since the end of the eighteenth century has been the whiter—and therefore more prestigious—wheat bread.

Russian peasants have remained very attached to their many varieties of black rye bread, usually in the shape of a round or rectangular loaf. Originally, rye from the field was ground by hand with the double stone disk mill to be found on every farm, but this was hard work. The flour could also be brought to the mill for grinding. Home-ground flour produced black bread, while the miller's wheat flour resulted in a bran bread from sifted flour, or a white bread without bran, if the grain's husk had been separated by the grindstones before milling. Rye bread has been an object of great respect in Russia and many traditions are associated with it. Neither wheat nor white bread inspire such devotion: white wheat bread, a recent import, is viewed as a form of cake, a non-essential luxury. It is eaten as a treat at Christmas, at Easter, or to celebrate marriages and births. But the white bread baked with salt in city bakeries is not particularly popular.

The peasant women of Byelorussia impart a delicious flavor to their rye bread by baking it on a bed of maple or oak leaves. The leaves are gathered in the fall, strung up to dry, and stored in large sacks, one sack of oak leaves, one of maple, to ensure good bread all winter. After Easter, fresh horseradish leaves are put to the same use, and so are fresh green cabbage leaves in the Fall. A comparable custom still existed recently in France, around Evreux, and in Northern Portugal, where traditional corn bread, or *broa,* was baked on eucalyptus leaves.

Northern countries with cold climates favored unleavened rye bread, very dense and suitable for long storage. It was disk shaped with a hole in the middle, and hung from the house rafters to last all winter. In Sweden, Finland, Iceland, and Denmark, tradition required that this bread be decorated with circular designs. In Northern Sweden, it is said, reindeer blood was kneaded with a little barley and a great deal of water. The gruel that resulted would be cooked on a flat stone until it hardened. In Estonia, the ingredients that were used to produce a similar gruel included rye scraps and pork blood. These flatbreads could remain "edible" for years. In the Alps, the isolation of which may be compared to that of the snowbound Northern regions of Scandinavia, the inhabitants felt the same need to prepare rye bread at the onset of winter and make it last through the hard season. These breads consisted of thick rye disks, only lightly risen from the use of natural yeast. The oven in which they were baked is the same everywhere: a direct-heat, wood-fueled oven, the age-old country oven of Europe.

In Switzerland, bread of this type is still made in several valleys of the Valais region. The menfolk of each family knead the rye dough in long wooden troughs, adding starter yeast from fermented dough. After fermentation, the dough is shaped into disks, and before it is allowed to rest, it is incised according to a specific code for each family so that the loaves can be identified after baking. The shaped loaves are carried by the men on a portable rack to the village's communal oven, where they are all baked together. Stored in a special place reserved for them, these loaves can be eaten all winter long.

Above: **Rye bread from the Valais region, Switzerland.**

THE SYMBOLISM OF BREAD

With its rich symbolism, bread embodies the traditions and beliefs of nations. Associated with the gods of most religions and with many sacred rites, since time immemorial it has attended the great events of various human communities: monsoon or grape harvest bread, the blessed bread of Catholics or the unleavened bread of Jewish Passover, or the fasting-break bread of Ramadan. There is no bread that does not, somewhere in the world, celebrate an agricultural or religious holiday, enrich a family event, or commemorate the dead. With prayers and offerings, responding to the cadence of the seasons, the religious aspect of bread is intended to appease the sometimes protective, sometimes temperamental divinities.

In traditional societies, for instance, each stage of life is represented by a specific bread— from birth to funerals, from marriage to childbirth. The aspects and events of our social and religious lives demonstrate the mythical quality of bread, and by ensuring and symbolizing the survival of the human race down through the ages, bread has become a part of the cycle of life.

Left: **Clever Tom Thumb, whose mean parents tried to abandon him in the woods, scatters bread crumbs to find his way back.**

Right: *The Baker's Shop,* **with the Saint-Nicholas** *cougnou* **bread. Oil on wood, Job Adriensz Berckheyde (1630–1693).**

BREAD OF SAINT NICHOLAS

In Europe, the Day of Saint Nicholas on December 6 marks the beginning of the children's festival. Perched on his mule, Old Saint Nicholas makes his rounds, bringing gifts and cakes to good little children, while his inseparable companion, Père Fouettard, is the bogeyman who threatens to deal with the naughty ones.

Throughout Eastern France and Switzerland (in Zurich and Saint-Gall), parents traditionally give their children little gingerbreads decorated with a colored image that represents Saint Nicholas and his gifts. In Alsace, offerings include *springerle,* or anise rolls, shaped in wooden molds such as those that can be seen at the Musée Alsacien (1800).

In Belgium, Holland, Switzerland, and Germany, Saint Nicholas and Père Fouettard are eaten as *speculoos,* delicious shortcake cookies shaped in hollow wooden molds. The Collard factory in Dinant makes wheat flour and honey specialties called *couques,* intended more to be admired than eaten, showing the good bishop holding his miter and staff, and dressed in his ceremonial garb. Nowadays, with the pre-eminence of Christmas, in response to commercial pressures, the image of Saint Nicholas on the gingerbread is slowly but surely changing into a rather strange white-bearded Father Christmas riding his mount, a Father Christmas who still wears the bishop's tiara but who already carries a basket full of presents. Fortunately, Saint Nicholas has not been entirely forgotten: the fair held in Strasbourg from December 4 to 24, sells both Saint Nicholas and Christmas gingerbreads.

Left: **Bishop Saint Nicholas preparing for his rounds.** *Couque* **from Dinant, Belgium.**

Printen, shortbreads shaped in old wooden molds: the Holy Family, carriages, angel, and Saint-Nicholas. Aachen, Germany.

Bread Men

The feast of Saint Nicholas on December 6 encompasses its share of children's visions and legends. A well-remembered and still active tradition is to represent Saint Nicholas in the form of a good-natured, rather roughly fashioned figure, made of milk bread. He is called a *cougnou* in Walloon Belgium, *kerst broden* in Flemish, *bubbe* or *männle* in Alsace, *mannli, fräauli* or *grittibänz* in German-speaking Switzerland. In Germany, the figure is sometimes represented rather oddly, smoking a pipe. At other times, in Lausanne for example, the character is very stylized and goes by the name of *bonhomme Saint Nicolas,* or more rarely, *tronche.* So goes the unfathomable maze of languages and semantics.

The meaning of these milk bread puppets offered to children has surely changed according to time and place. Thus, for the bakers of Brussels, the *cougnou* wearing little raisins for buttons represents the Baby Jesus. In the North of France, people talk about *P'tit Jésus,* Lil' Jesus figures. In Provence, on December 26, the day after Christmas (Saint Etienne's name day), godparents used to make bread dough figures, called *estève* or *pain de Saint-Etienne,* enriched with sugar and olive oil, to give to their godchild. Similar bread figurines were made at home in the Languedoc and the Ardèche, where they were known as *Père Janvier, couloun,* or *coulon.* And in French Canada, in the 1950s, little girls still received dolls called *catin,* made of cooked bread dough, as Christmas presents. These were sometimes enigmatic traditions, open to fancy, as befits the legend of Saint Nicholas resuscitating three little children who had had their throats cut and were preserved in salt by a sausage maker.

Left: **Jan Steen,** *Saint Nicholas Celebration,* **seventeenth century. Amsterdam, Rijksmuseum.**

CHRISTMAS CELEBRATIONS

Christmas is an occasion for religious festivities and for children to help their mothers prepare special breads, such as cumin bread in Denmark, or anise bread in Gascony. Swedish children amuse themselves by building bread and cookie houses decorated with candied fruit, to be eaten with great gusto after the children have played with them to their hearts' content. This tradition recalls the Grimm fairy tale of *Hansel and Gretel,* in which two children are abandoned by their parents, who are too poor to raise them; Hansel finds himself locked up by a witch in a bread house, but Gretel manages to free her brother and they both devour the house to make their escape.

Among the unusual breads made at Christmastime is one from the region of Werratal in Germany, which symbolizes the winter solstice: it is shaped like a horseshoe decorated with a serpent and images of the solar months. In Alsace, the bread served at the family meal is a pear bread, the *bierewecke.* And the Musée Alsacien contains examples of admirable Christmas gingerbreads made in Strasbourg in the early seventeenth century, shaped in a baked-clay mold and representing the Virgin seated with the Christ-Child.

Christmas bread, like those associated with other religious celebrations, may naturally represent a sacred symbol. In Provence, the Christmas bread is round, studded with four walnuts arranged as a cross. An olive branch bearing fruit used to be placed in the middle. Custom required that it be kept on the family table until Epiphany, to bring abundance to the house.

In many regions, Christmas Eve is devoted to making the breads and brioches to be eaten after Midnight Mass. In Brittany, the meal ends with the traditional star-shaped *fouace.* In Lille, the Christmas brioche is called a *coquille.* In the Ardèche, fritters are served, and in Lorraine, there is a braided brioche called *tordé.* In Provence, it would be a big bread made with olive oil, which is not touched until one-quarter of it has been given to the first poor person met on the road, a charitable obligation. Before leaving for Midnight Mass, churchgoers fortify themselves with a fish soup, accompanied by the famous *fougasse,* one of thirteen other cakes and grain desserts.

Some customs have been lost, such as the Haute-Provence tradition of carefully collecting the crumbs from Christmas bread to scatter in the fields, in the hope of ensuring a good crop. Elsewhere, new customs have been adopted: Londoners were introduced a few years ago to heart-shaped gingerbreads (imported from Germany) inscribed with a "Merry Xmas" in white icing surrounded by flowers. In Italy, the familiar wheat and raisin Christmas brioche called *panettone* is now mass produced.

Christmas trees have been a tradition for more than a century, and they are decorated throughout Eastern Europe with various rolls and gingerbreads: in Russia, little mint-flavored buns, knights, and birds; in Germany, cookies shaped like moons, stars, and braids. In Vienna, during the month before Christmas, souvenir shops behind Saint Stephen's Cathedral sell squirrel, dove, and other bird figures to hang on the tree. These decorations are made of very hard bread dough. The Austrian capital also hosts a fair where gingerbread is a special feature.

Opposite: **The gingerbread house decorated with pretzels where the witch tried to lock up Hansel and Gretel. Popular lithograph.**

Below: **Baked hard-flour dough figurine for Christmas tree decoration. Vienna.**

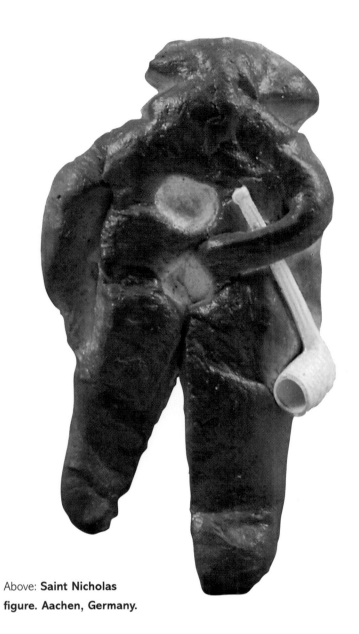

Above: **Saint Nicholas
figure. Aachen, Germany.**

Above: **Christmas bread:
Sun and Moon. Eastern
Serbia.**

Right: **The three little children
brought back to life by Saint
Nicholas.** *Couque* from
Dinant, Belgium.

Santons and Bread

The *santons,* those traditional figures which adorn Christmas crèches in Provence, were originally made not of baked clay but of bread dough, and were placed in churches to await Christmas night. The Musée du Vieux Marseille has a collection of *santons* made of colored bread. Nativity scenes peopled with multicolored bread figures are also to be found in Italy, with the Christ Child in the manger, the Virgin Mary, Saint Joseph, and musicians and birds. They are also popular in the Czech Republic, where they are made of bread and paper pulp in Svatá Hora, near Pribam.

Below: **Painted and glazed bread figurines for Nativity scenes. Ecuador.**

The custom of modeling bread dough into various Nativity characters has spread through South America. However, it is in Ecuador that Nativity bread figures are now most commonly found. They may well be descendants of those figurines made of bread dough that were placed on parents' graves on the day of the dead. Just as the Nativity figures of Provence represent local characters dressed in the regional garb of their time, their Ecuadorian counterparts are modeled after the Indians of the region. All these figures are brightly painted and varnished. The *santons* have multiplied as a result of tourist demand, mutating into animals, multicolored turtles, or red roses on their stems, subjects which no longer have anything to do with Nativity scenes.

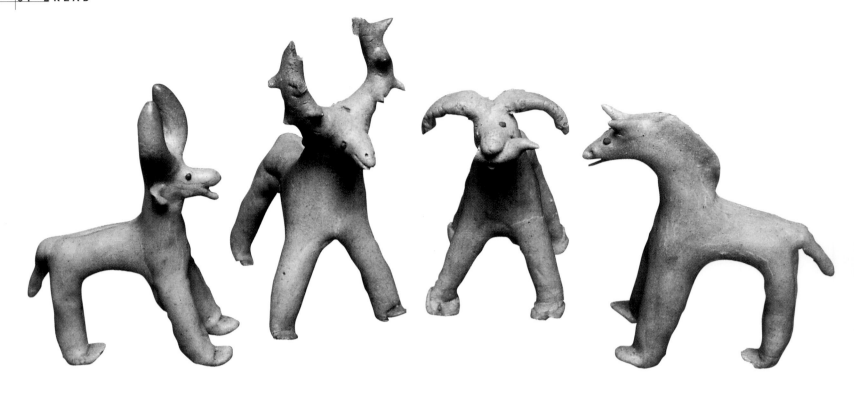

NEW YEAR CELEBRATIONS

On the first of January, the peasant women of Central Europe used to make ritual breads that were intended to have a magical function: to ensure the renewal of fertility and to foster growth. These breads often portray idyllic scenes of farm life. In Bulgaria, large round breads illustrate the coming harvest with its wheat sheaves and its haystacks. In other examples, a whole microcosm of the domestic world is prepared on New Year's Eve: the sheepfold with the ewes, the lambs, and the ram, the plow and the plowhand, the wheat field and the haystacks, the threshing floor, the dog. These breads are made of wheat flour which the youngest woman of the household sifts three times. The mistress of the house kneads the dough using silent, untouched, flowered water (*silent* because the young bride who fetches it from the fountain must speak to no one on her way, *untouched* because no one would dare drink from it, and *flowered* because magic herbs have been thrown into the pail).[7] The bread is decorated either by hand or through the use of women's implements such as a spindle or a thimble. In Poland, the ritual New Year's Day bread is made "so that the cattle will prosper": it represents the farm woman tending her geese, or sometimes a sculpted deer

symbolically enfolding the sun within its horns according to ancient tradition. In Eastern Europe, bread could also be an element of divination.

In Sweden, Denmark, and Austria, the New Year was celebrated with breads shaped like the ancient swastika, a cross with spiraling tips that symbolized nature's renewal and the transition to another year. In Germany there was also bread shaped like a hooked cross, representing the tree of life as the emblem of the New Year, with the new growth to come, bringing heavenly blessings.

Beyond cultural differences, a consistent symbolism surfaces among certain Asian people. In Iran, the New Year is always celebrated at the moment from which it should never have been displaced, on the first day of the spring solstice (March 21 or 22). This is when the celebration exemplifies its true sense of the renewal of nature and vegetation: families gather at home to herald the New Year around a big fragrant flatbread sprinkled with poppy, sesame, cardamom, or black cumin seed *(nigella sativa)*.

The Alevis of Anatolia still observe a New Year's festival that can be traced to the ancient Turks, the Hizir Festival, named for a god of water and greenery, and held during the Calends of February.

Above: **Bread dough sun-symbol animal figures for the New Year. Ostroleka, near Warsaw, Poland.**

Below: **Lady and gentleman, molded in an eighteenth-century tradition, originating respectively from Vienna, Austria, and Torun, Poland.**

"After a three-day fast, people purify themselves, go to the baths, and put on clean, preferably white clothing. On Thursday night, they lay out a white tablecloth and spread flour on it; the next morning, if a horseshoe-shaped mark can be seen on the flour, it means that *Hizir Nebi* has entered the house, and this flour is immediately used to bake a ritual bread called *köme* or *kömme,* which is distributed."[8] By observing this custom, the people start the year anew, white and purified through fasting and ritual, ready to receive the blessings of the divinity and of nature.

Northern China has a special sort of steamed New Year roll called *mantou.* These wheat flour buns are inscribed with red or black edible ink characters meaning "happiness," "double happiness," or "prosperity."

Tibetan nomads had a longevity bread, made of four braided strips of dough and fried in oil, which was a good portent for the coming year, since oil is a luxury. A similar tradition persists among the Mongols: at the beginning of the New Year or "white month" *(tsagaansar),* families gather in the *yurt,* the portable round dwelling of Central Asian shepherds, and share a long wheat loaf *(ul boov)* decorated with a carved wooden stamp, and fried in mutton fat—which here again symbolizes wealth and prosperity. Similarly, on the White Feast Day, May 9, the lamas at the Gandan monastery receive trays filled with five stacked layers of these decorated rolls paying tribute to "the White Elder, Master of the Earth, Highest of Tutelary Divinities."[9]

Above: **Bread bike offered as a birthday present. Paris.**

Above: **Bread representing Saint Lazarus resuscitated by Jesus. Kos Island, Greece.**

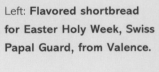

Left: **Flavored shortbread for Easter Holy Week, Swiss Papal Guard, from Valence.**

Above: **Birthday bread in the form of a mask. Montreuil-sous-bois.**

Right: **Biscuit from Aachen, Germany.**

Left: **Shortbread from Aachen, Germany.**

Right: **New Year's bread, symbol of eternity. Morocco.**

Above: **Portrait-bread offered as a birthday present. Amsterdam.**

Above: **Decorative crocodile. Saint-Etienne.**

FROM EPIPHANY TO APRIL FOOL'S DAY

Epiphany falls on the first Sunday after New Year's day, when the Magi, guided by the Star of Bethlehem, brought their gifts to the newborn Christ. This is when families share a special cake containing a hidden dry bean—or a golden coin when possible. The one who finds it becomes king for the day.

In Provence and throughout Southwestern France, this cake is not the ubiquitous pastry cream *galette,* but rather a crown-shaped brioche bread called a *royaume.* This tradition of the *galette des rois* is so deeply rooted in France that it has become official: every year, representatives of the bakers' profession come to the Élysée Palace to offer a *galette* to the President of the Republic. One month later, at Candlemas, wheat flour is once again associated with the wish for abundance, as families gather to share the traditional crêpes. In the French countryside, respect for this custom held the promise of a robust wheat or other grain harvest.

It was also said that eating the crêpes would bring luck, prosperity, and money during the coming year. Thus children used to go around neighboring farms asking for eggs and flour to make the crêpes, which they would flip while holding a *sou* in order to "be rich all year." A pious wish? Perhaps, but the custom later spread to the middle class, where a gold coin replaced the *sou.* Similar rituals were observed across the English Channel, where eating crêpes was also a spring fertility rite involving a gold coin held in the hand when flipping the pancake.

Mardi Gras, celebrated on the day before Lent begins, is the next occasion for eating crêpes or fritters, with the same original intent of ensuring prosperity and abundant crops. In Macedonia there is still a special cake called *lagana,* eaten on Fat Monday. As in ancient times, this is an unleavened cake cooked on a hot griddle.

The Lenten period which precedes Easter is traditionally a forty-day fast. But there are compromises: while some foods such a meats must be given up, others fill the gap so that hearty eaters will not be too deprived. In Flaubert's *Madame Bovary,* for instance, Madame Homais consoles herself with the Lenten rolls called *cheminots,* found in Rouen. The commitment that the faithful undertake to fast makes bread more indispensable than ever at mealtime. In Alsace, during Lent, pretzels are made without butter *(faschtebretzstell).* During the forty days of fasting before Easter, Orthodox Christians eat plain slices of bread sprinkled with olive oil.

Lastly, April Fool's Day, known in France as "the fishes of April," commemorates what used to be the beginning of the year: Easter is not always over by April 1st, which means that the Lenten fasting period has not always ended. On that day, people eat shortbread cookies in the shape of fishes, or as in Saint-Etienne, flaky pastry shaped like fish.

Above: **Fish for the Lenten season, when eating meat is forbidden.** *Couque* **from Dinant, Belgium.**

EASTER BREADS

Easter celebrates the resurrection of Christ, but it also celebrates fertility, and the season of renewal. Nature is reborn after the death of winter, and the Christian festival has evolved from pagan celebrations without ever quite eliminating them. Palm Sunday, heralding the beginning of Holy Week, commemorates the triumphal entry of Christ into Jerusalem, covered in olive branches like a tree full of life. But, above all, this final Sunday of Lent is a Church-approved occasion to prepare for Easter by bringing home, as in former pagan times, a green bough which has triumphed over winter. Better yet, safe from the charge of paganism, the Church blesses these boughs. Everywhere in the South of France, children bring them to Palm Sunday Mass to be blessed: they can be quite elaborate, trimmed with flowers, ribbons, and colored paper. The laurel branches are decorated with *gimblettes,* small rings of bread dough enriched with sugar and olive oil, and baked, as well as animal and plant figures, or according to a custom still followed in Sisteron, little bread men. These bread figures recall the Saint Nicholas and Christmas figures of the Northern regions; they go by various names: *estève* in Provence, *coulom* in the Ardèche, and *pantin* in the Haute-Loire near Saint-Etienne, where they are sold during Holy Week.

Further north, the church blesses branches of boxwood or holly. In Alsace, these branches are hung with *butterbretzstell* (butter pretzels), which are eaten at home after they have been blessed. In Charentes, the children's boughs hold *cornelles,* small triangular rolls covered with brushed egg yolk and aniseed.

Below: **Braided Easter breads, with fertility eggs. Greece.**

Bread and eggs—another powerful fertility symbol—are associated among the Mediterranean's Christian communities during their Easter celebrations. To this day, they make a brioche bread with an egg in the center as a symbol of the Resurrection. This Easter bread is usually braided, and contains a hard-boiled egg, dyed red for fertility, symbolizing the Resurrection of Christ.

In Nice, this Easter bread, called *échaudé,* has practically disappeared, except perhaps in the old section of town. It is shaped in the form of a circle with a red egg on top, or as a figure 8 embellished with an egg. But it can still be found in Corsica under the names of *campanili* in Bastia, *caccaveli* in Ajaccio, or *courcoun* in Bonifacio. In Calabria, the big bread crowns called *cuzzupa* contain one egg for each family member. The *titola* of Istria, and the *colombina* of Trieste and Northern Yugoslavia, are long, braided loaves garnished with an egg dyed red. In Greece, there is a crown-shaped version called *koulouri.* On the island of Corfu, the special Easter Bread may be trimmed with hen feathers dyed red, green, or purple. In Rhodes, the egg is colored green and set in the center of the braid; its name here is *tsoureki.* Elsewhere, it may be decorated with a cross and bird design between each branch, or with a human figure, but always with the red boiled egg in the center. The French in Algeria used to make an Easter brioche *(amouna)* with an egg dyed green with spinach juice (a specialty among Catholics of the Constantinois region).

Other Easter breads are still braided but are not topped with an egg, as in the Southern Tyrol, where some bakeries still offer a crown braided from three or four strands of dough, which is traditionally presented by godparents to their godchild.

The Armenians make a braided egg bread, the *tcheurek,* prepared with flour, water, eggs, oil, milk, *salep* (orchid bulb flour), sugar, a little salt, and some yeast.

Madame Homais was very fond of the heavy turban-shaped rolls eaten during Lent with salted butter, last vestige of the gothic foods dating back perhaps to the century of the crusades, rolls with which the sturdy Normans stuffed themselves, believing that in the light of yellow torches, between the tankards of hyppocras and the monumental meats, they were seeing on their table the heads of Saracens to be devoured.

(Gustave Flaubert, *Madame Bovary*)

In Northern Italy, one can still find dove-shaped Easter bread stamps used to prepare a specialty egg bread called the "Easter Dove," which is now made by commercial bakeries. In Monaco, for Easter as well as Christmas, a crown-shaped *fougace* is made with a topping of grains dyed yellow or blue.

For Easter Sunday, Orthodox Christians dye and decorate eggs. On Holy Thursday to commemorate the Last Supper, when Christ shared bread with his disciples, they prepare in absolute silence a brioche or egg bread called *koulitch.* On the Saturday night of Resurrection, they walk in procession to church with a basket of eggs, holding a candle in one hand, and the bread in the other. They exchange a kiss and ask each other's forgiveness for any offense they might have committed against one another, as a token of peace for the future.

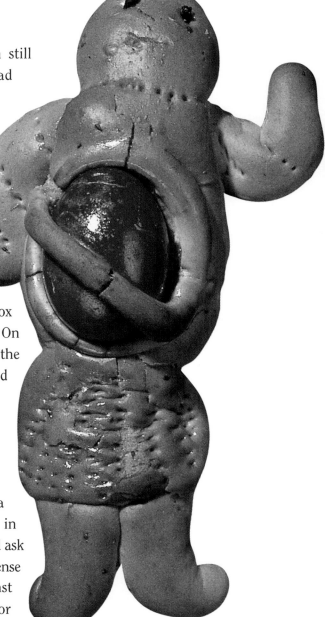

Above: **Brioche bread enclosing an egg, symbol of the Resurrection of Christ. Greece.**

Opposite: **Orthodox wedding bread. Karpathos Island, Greece.**

Unleavened Passover Bread

The ceremony of Pesach, or Passover, celebrates the flight of the Jewish people from Egypt and the beginning of their forty years of wandering in the desert; but it also signifies rebirth and their departure toward the Promised Land.

In commemoration, God commands his people: "Seven days shall ye eat unleavened bread; even the first day ye shall put away leaven out of your houses: for whosoever eateth leavened bread from the first day until the seventh day, that soul shall be cut off from Israel" *(Exodus, XII, 15)*. Nowhere in the Bible is there an explanation concerning this prohibition against eating leavened bread during the week of Passover. As for the mandatory unleavened bread, it only specifies that the Hebrews "baked unleavened cakes of the dough which they brought forth out of Egypt, for it was not leavened; because they were thrust out of Egypt, and could not tarry, neither had they prepared for themselves any victual" *(Exodus, XII, 39)*. The bread dough they carried would surely have had time to rise before mealtime, but by divine edict, the Jews returned to the status of shepherds following their flocks, and nomads have no bread ovens but must cook their *unleavened* flatbread on a griddle or flat stone. The unleavened bread thus does not commemorate the exodus from Egypt, but the wandering in the desert imposed by God as a punishment on his people for having betrayed Him.

This unleavened bread has another religious significance: it is the bread which God demands as an offering, the twelve *pains de proposition,* or showbreads, whose number and quality are exactingly specified. The Bible frequently mentions this unleavened bread made of "fine wheat flour" (often kneaded or sprinkled with oil) and offered up to God. Unleavened bread is the purest, the whitest of breads, just as the communion wafer is white, pure, unleavened. Yeast is a foreign body, an impurity that induces fermentation, synonymous with defilement: the dough is relinquished to obscure forces which act upon it.

During the entire celebration of Passover, therefore, Jewish bakeries stop making bread and even the presence of leavening is prohibited. Jews eat the ritual unleavened flatbread, *matzos.* When they can, Jewish communities make their own, to be certain that the rules are respected. The Hassidic communities of Antwerp, Montreal, and Boston for instance, prepare at least the three flatbreads *(matse-mitsve)* of the Passover meal of the first two evenings, the Seder. "The symbolic Seder dish is placed at the center of the table: it consists of three flatbreads, each covered with a napkin, along with various symbolic dishes, the bitter herbs, a braised bone, and so on. The two Seder meals thus require six unleavened breads."[10]

The rules for preparing these flatbreads are stipulated in detail in the sixteenth-century *Code of Jewish Laws.* But nowadays they are baked in the oven, which is the domain of leavened dough, rather than on the original griddle. Similarly, the oft-repeated Biblical injunction for the twelve showbreads (also called *face breads*) to be deposited in Jehovah's sanctuary, is no longer observed, except among Tunisian Jews who developed the custom of placing weekly offerings of square breads stacked "one on top of the other and separated for airing by little golden cylinders."[11]

Except for these communities, the unleavened flatbreads are industrially produced under rabbinical supervision. In France, some are imported from Israel, but most of them are made by the S. Bitone factory, "La Bienfaisante," in Agen, Lot-et-Garonne, "according to the recipes used in Algeria," as well as by Rosinski at Neuilly-sur-Marne, or the Neymann Company, established in 1850.

Opposite: **Passover matzos. Israel.**

WEDDING BREADS

Once the sweethearts have found each other, and the match has been arranged by the parents, all that remains is to marry the lovers!

The richest traditions associated with wedding bread come from Central Europe and the Balkans. The young bride must be protected at all costs from the evil eye, and all must be done to ensure prosperity and happiness for the newlyweds. The nuptial bread and its rituals are one of the essential elements in a Slavic wedding, whether it be in Russia, Byelorussia, the Ukraine, or Bulgaria. "The dough is made, decorated, and the bread that will be offered to the wedding guests is baked. This is accompanied by numerous rituals and songs in which the bread is compared to the sun and the moon. The betrothed bow deeply to the bread and kiss it. The parents bless the young couple and greet them with bread and salt when they return from church, as if to pass on the traditions of Slavic hospitality; they shower the bride and groom with grains of wheat, to wish them happiness and wealth."[12]

In nineteenth-century Bulgaria, in Greece, and in Yugoslavia, bread was as essential to marriage celebrations as to religious observances, or to those ceremonies associated with the agricultural calendar. Outside the church, after the wedding, the godparents stand alongside the newlyweds, holding a loaf of bread wrapped in a white cloth to bring them prosperity.

In Poland and the Ukraine, the bread presented at the wedding feast is particularly beautiful. It is round, adorned with about ten long stalks, each bearing a dove or a flower. The plants and birds symbolize fertility. The blooming stalks represent the trees which connect heaven and earth, and allow blessings to descend from above, while the dove is the sign of the Holy Spirit bringing divine blessing to humankind. These traditional marriage loaves, called *karowaj* or *kolacz,* are still made in Rezeszow and Bialystok.

In Cracow, similar figures made of hardened bread decorate the marriage bread: a dove on a bough or surrounded with flowers, a pair of doves with their eggs or kissing, or sometimes a horse-shoe surmounted by a rose—a more modern symbol but one with the same significance.

The tree and dove symbolism is even more apparent in Moravia. Here, the wedding bread is topped with a spray of paper leaves on branches, sometimes 75 centimeters high, which rests on a base of baked dough. The branches are filled with baked bread birds, little egg bread rolls, or amazing figurines. Sometimes the piece includes gingerbread motifs such as horses, birds, or swaddled babies decorated with colored sugar, crowned with a gingerbread heart or a doll representing the bride.

These dough figurines are hardened in the oven after having been immersed in hot water. They have been so successful at Christmas and

Opposite: **Ceremonial marriage bread. Hungary.**

Below: **Sculpted crown for wedding feast. Crete.**

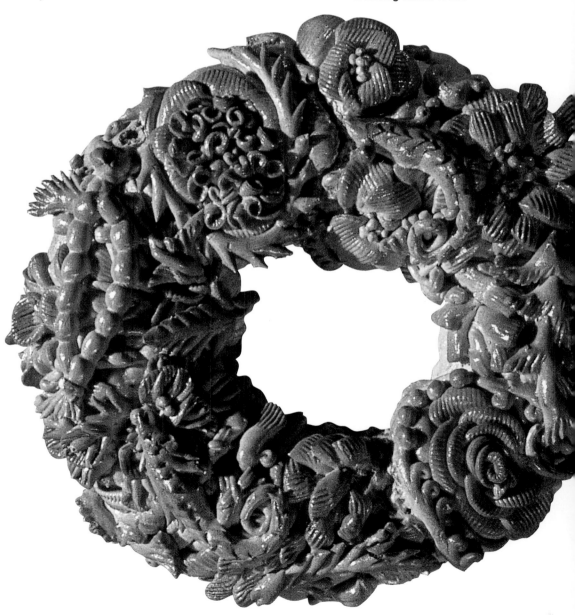

145

Easter fairs that their fabrication has expanded significantly. One of the most beautiful of these creations represents Adam and Eve on either side of the Tree of Knowledge, with the serpent of temptation coiled around the trunk. This echoes the familiar Eurasian art theme of animals surrounding the tree of life. But there are many other motifs: the groom-to-be as a knight, or the future bride on horseback, wearing her large bonnet; an infant in swaddling clothes; a siren, birds, doves, ducks, a fish, a lizard—not to mention all the married couples standing side by side with their hands on their hips. The town of Vizovice, in Valasko, is the main production center for these marriage-bread figures; the Lutonsky shop has the best reputation and has created a great many variations on the traditional themes. This custom has been adopted in neighboring Austria, and little doves and other Christmas tree decorations of baked

dough are on display around St. Stephen's Cathedral in Vienna at Christmas time. Bulgaria has also started to produce these figures, usually in various animal shapes of more modern design.

The wedding bread in Slovakia is less stylized but just as ornate. It is a round loaf with a likeness of the couple sculpted on the surface before baking: the man wearing his hat, the woman her bonnet, and with them, the naked baby that they soon will have. The interlaced volute and double volute designs are an expression of a solar symbolism.

In Greece, Macedonia, and Crete, an enormous wedding bread is carried in on someone's head, to be eaten at the wedding feast. The dough for this bread is kneaded seven times, and its leavening is obtained from a mixture of crushed chickpeas and water that had been left to ferment. The bread is shaped like the round pan in which it was baked, and it is elaborately decorated.

In the Islamic world, the bread associated with marriage has much the same symbolic meaning as in Central Europe: to bring fertility, prosperity, happiness, and abundance. The shared bread also seals the agreement between the young couple

Below: **Hare-shaped bread offered to boys by their godfathers on All Saints' Day. Tyrol, Austria.**

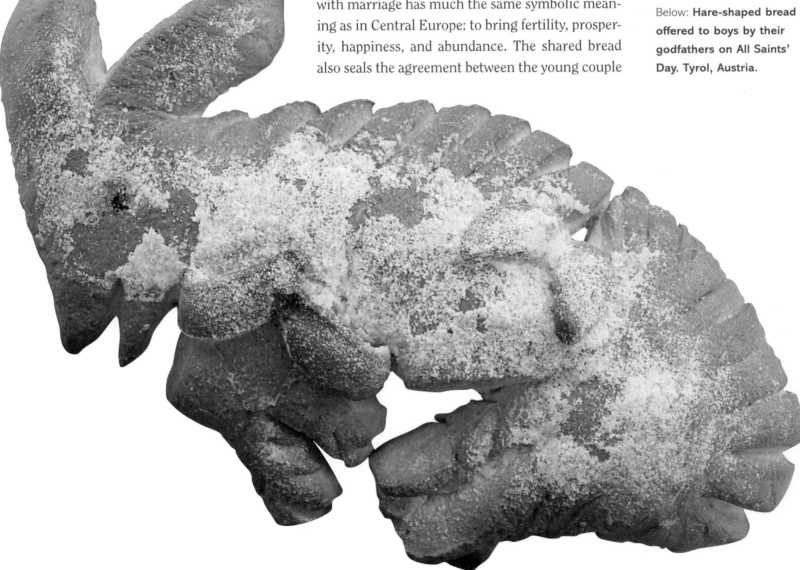

and the families, and signifies the acceptance of the young bride into her new family.

In Central Asia, the whole village comes to share in the wedding feast—if the host can afford it. Everyone brings specially baked breads, sugared flat cakes, sweets, and fruit. Among the Uzbeks of Afghanistan, the family distributes squares of dough fried in oil and candies to all the guests. Since the young woman will be leaving her father's house to live with her new husband, and must sometimes move quite far from her native village, she carries with her a loaf of bread as a memento of the happy days of her youth and as a link to the world of her childhood.

Among the Turkomans of Central Asia, the bride is led with great ceremony to her husband; she is resplendently bejeweled, bearer of her father's glory, and seated on the ceremonial dromedary. She is followed by the caravan that carries her yurt, her entire dowry, and a large flatbread baked by her mother in the family oven and wrapped in a beautiful silk or embroidered felt cover, the *boqtché,* whose four corners are folded in toward the middle. Here again, the bread represents her origins, which she takes along with her and which are meant to ensure her happiness in her new life.

Among the Patchounes of Afghanistan, at the moment of the marriage itself, i.e., the exchange of mutual consent before witnesses, the couple about to marry is seated side-by-side, covered by a veil. Before them is an open copy of the Koran, and a mirror. When the veil is removed, the betrothed look at each other for the first time, in that mirror. They then read a verse from the Koran, and the groom offers the bride a piece of bread covered with sesame seeds, which she eats; in turn, she offers him a cup of water, which he drinks. If they laugh at that moment, they will be happy in their marriage, and wheat will be inexpensive during the year.

Above: **Hanging straw ornament decorated with communion wafers, kept in the house to bring prosperity. Poland.**

Left: **Crowned cupid, bearer of happiness.** *Couque* from Dinant, Belgium.

147

FUNERAL BREAD

In celebrating the day of the dead, many countries and many people honor the echo of funeral rites of long ago, of those recurring absolutions of boiled grain for the dead, of those ancient joyful graveside meals to which the Ancestors are invited: customs meant to associate the dead with the life of the community, to distract them while showing them that they have not been forgotten, that they are still part of our lives. The tradition of offering bread to the departed still endures in some regions of France: it takes place during a wake on the eve of November 2, and may be the reason why All Saints' Day, which is also the day honoring all the saints and ancestors, a day celebrated by the Catholic church on November 1,

Opposite: **Communion of the living and the dead. Festival of the Dead in Mexico.**

Below: *Festival of the Dead in Mexico.* **Mural painting, Diego Rivera.**

at the beginning of the Celtic year, has become essentially the day of the dead (All Souls' Day), which normally would not be celebrated until the next day. In Corsica, the "invocation of the dead" involves various offerings such as the *canistrelli,* a sort of little crown flavored with anise. In Bastia, crown-shaped anise cookies called *salviate* serve to celebrate All Saints' Day. In the Finisterre, in Plougastel and Daoualas, a blessed bread called "souls' bread" is similarly offered to the dead. Not long ago, during the burial mass, parishioners took turns offering blessed bread, often a brioche glazed with egg. "It was elongated, fairly large, with rounded corners, and marked with a cross in the center. The children of the choir used to cut it in the sacristy and distribute it in a basket before the Offertory. It was eaten right in church."[13] The custom of distributing blessed bread at the conclusion of the mass has endured longest in connection with burials. This ritual was also observed during what Catholics call "the year's end service," the mass celebrated in church one year after someone's death, particularly in the Sancerre region.

Funeral Banquets

Among Orthodox Christians, bread is intimately associated with death—at the moment of death, during the funeral ceremonies, and during the collective observances that take place on Easter Sunday.

"Food for the dead," called *kolyva* or *zito,* made of boiled wheat with crushed walnuts and honey sprinkled with flour, is an old Balkan tradition. "It is prepared for all burial ceremonies and all commemorative funeral observances. On those occasions, it is first brought to the church in a receptacle reserved for this purpose, and it is blessed by the priest. Later, at the cemetery, after some of it has been offered to the dead, it is shared among all those present."[14] These funeral banquets still take place. In Russia, after prayers are said at the cemetery, a dish is passed around and everyone, in turn, eats a spoonful.

Mexico's *Pan de Muertos:*

Bread of the Dead

The day of the dead is celebrated in Mexico with equal fervor by everyone, whether of native or mixed ancestry, in the towns and in the country. On November 1 and 2, the dead return to visit the living and each family must receive its dead with "flowers of the dead," *cempoalxochitl,* along with food and drink, which are offered at the grave as well as at the home altar.

The departed loved ones are greeted with a smile, and their day is a cheerful festival which has become an occasion to exchange gifts. Children receive toys relating to death: articulated skeletons, funeral processions, or *calaveras* (skulls), made of papier-mâché. The celebration has a gastronomy of its own. The brows of the sugar *calaveras* are marked with the names of the friends for whom they are intended. Another special treat during this period is the *pan de muertos,* the bread of the dead, a sugary wheat pastry with a flavor similar to brioche.

Such specialty breads are offered to the deceased, of course, but also to the living, both children and adults. Even in native villages where people normally eat corn tortillas but not bread, the bread of the dead appears during the first half of November and is included among gifts for honored friends.

The bread of the dead is becoming increasingly popular in the cities. It takes different forms: human bodies, tibias, even miniature mountains glazed with red sugar. Everybody buys them as presents.

In recent decades, during the period when the bread of the dead is sold, bakeries and pastry shops in major cities have demonstrated their seasonal creativity through elaborate window displays, thus developing a new form of popular visual art. The displays are filled with inscriptions and drawings proclaiming "Best Bread of the Dead Here," or "Delicious Bread of the Dead." Multicolored painted designs fill the remaining space. Skeleton characters act out scenes of daily life; others portray inherent urban situations such as mass transit; there might be a picture of a bus full of skeleton passengers, or modern-day adventures with skeleton astronauts.

Left: **Bread of the dead in a bakery window on November 2nd. Mexico.**

Ritual bread may also be shared during the burial, as in Greece or Bulgaria. It is a round loaf marked in the middle with a special stamp, as is the bread used in the Mass, with the inscription *IS, XS, NIKA,* "Jesus-Christ Victorious." This bread of the dead, which used to be made by the family of the deceased, is now ordered from a bakery for funerals and commemorative ceremonies held on the fortieth day, three months, or one year after the death. Blessed in church, the bread is then brought to the cemetery; the first piece is placed on the grave, and the rest is shared among those present. After returning to the village, one of the women in the family visits close friends in other families and brings them one of these breads.

In Serbia, the bread eaten at the graveside bears the same "Jesus-Christ Victorious" inscription in Cyrillic characters, *IC, XP, HIKA,* within a square divided into four by a cross. In Romania, the crown-shaped funeral breads are placed on the cart that carries the dead in an open coffin—an Orthodox tradition. These sacrificial breads, called *pomana,* are eaten by the family and neighbors of the deceased on his behalf, to give him strength to face the voyage to the hereafter.

Food of the Dead

The deceased does not immediately resign himself to leave the world of the living which he has loved. He looks back on it with nostalgia, not knowing exactly what awaits him in the beyond. And he is hungry. The living, therefore, leave food for him to eat right away and also to take with him, because the soul has a long way to go before reaching bliss. The ancient Egyptians used to place in their tombs loaves of bread in sealed copper vessels so that the deceased would not want for anything.

In Afghanistan, before Nuristan turned to Islam, women there would prepare flatbreads made with some fat to leave inside the raised wooden coffin containing the deceased, at the edge of the village. Now that the dead are buried instead of being left exposed, the custom continues among the non-Islamicized Kalash people of Pakistan: "The deceased is buried with his bow, and with a

goatskin bag containing bread, flour, and cheese."[15] The day after the funeral, the villagers come to throw pieces of flatbread and cheese on the grave, as a final meal for the deceased.

The Muslims are also familiar with the ritual of distributing unleavened bread among the faithful. Returning from the funeral, all those who accompanied the deceased on his last earthly journey share a communal meal in memory of the

Above: **Ceremony honoring the dead in Mexico. Painting by Diego Rivera.**

departed soul, who rejoices at the gaiety of this funeral banquet held in his honor. For a proper death there must be a lot of guests, so that people can talk forever after about "a beautiful funeral."

In Tunisia, bread and olives were distributed after the funeral. In Iran, on the evening of the second day, neighbors receive *halvah* (wheat flour fried in butter and mixed with sugar, saffron, and rose water), presented in a folded bread *(senguek),* or a loaf of spiced honey bread.

In Northern Afghanistan, the day after the funeral, the family offers all participants a square fritter made of flour and oil. For a rich family, the ritual is very specific. One man goes to market, where he buys 28 kg of sesame oil and 21 kg of brown sugar. Another man brings 224 kg of wheat, a full dromedary load, to be ground at the mill. Ten old village women sift the flour four or five times until it is absolutely pure. Then, they blend it with oil to make a dough which they flatten with a wooden rolling pin. With a knife, they cut the dough into squares which they fry in a kettle. In the meantime, the women have heated the brown sugar with water to make a caramel syrup which they pour over the pile of fritters, or *tchalpak.* These are carried from house to house by three men and three women who give each person in the house one fritter. After having said a prayer, the people consume the fritters in honor of the dead.

Bread Dolls

In South America, the cult of the dead is very much alive. As we know, the ancient Maya prepared the body of the deceased "as if for a trip: he was dressed in a traveler's tunic, with little pieces of jade and of dried flatbread placed in his mouth, all the things that must be provided for a traveler." [16] These customs of providing the dead with "travel provisions" were repressed by the missionaries, and when contemporary Mexican Indians place miniature corn cakes and a container of water in a tomb next to the body, they do so in secret.

The Indians also used to hold yearly ceremonies in honor of the dead, and these celebrations have been legitimized by the new Catholic

religion, simply by holding them on the day of the Catholic observance.

In the cemetery of Las Animas, for three years following someone's death, the Aymara Indians of Bolivia celebrate November 3 with great ceremonies in honor of the dead. On each anniversary, the soul of the deceased is supposed to return among the living: on his tomb, the family sets out a banquet with his favorite food and arranges wheat or corn flour figurines around it. These "bread dolls" usually have human forms—a man, a woman made of bread dough with a multicolored sugar head—or they may be in the shape of animals or crowns. They are eaten at the grave and distributed to the poor, who give thanks by reciting prayers in honor of the deceased. In Ecuador on All Saints' Day, colored bread figurines are arranged on the tombs by family members. The figures represent people from the village, animals, or plants. Tourism has altered the tradition somewhat, and the shapes have multiplied to the point where they may even include political figures. The Zapotec Indians of Southern Mexico also adorn their tombs with bread characters whose heads have been molded out of colored dough. These heads are sold at the Oaxaca market on the day of the dead.

Left: **Invocation to the dead in a Romanian village. The lights are a link between the living and the dead.**

153

The Bread of Life

Bread has long been associated with the memory of the dead. Consecrated bread was once distributed to worshipers at the church door, in remembrance of the departed. Funeral bread was shared after the funeral, before the family members went their separate ways. And, in medieval times, alms bread was given as a gesture of Christian charity to the destitute, in commemoration of the dead.

This consecration of bread has generated many a ceremony and popular ritual, most of them forgotten now. The *Distribution du pain au village (Distribution of Bread in the Village)* is a quasi-ethnographic illustration of a custom still known in late-nineteenth-century Flemish country, particularly in Campine, where tradition required that bread be given to the poor when a rich villager died. This gesture, associating bread with the remembrance of the dead, also expresses the collective will to survive when faced with the loss of one of its members. Through this ritualistic act, the village community reaffirms its cohesion and its identity.

In their own way, these funeral breads are breads of life, earthly nourishment endowed with protective powers, left in the guise of a talisman. There is no doubt that the bread carried by the solemn and determined young village woman in the foreground of the painting is there not only as the promise of a meal, but also as an expression of the hopes and future of a community.

Left: **Frans Van Leemputten,** *Bread Distribution in the Village,* 1892. Antwerp, Musée royal des Beaux-Arts.

Sexual Symbolism of Bread

Bread-making has inspired countless sexual metaphors and references—the kneading of the dough, the leavening that makes it expand, the loading of the oven—but the shapes of certain breads actually are sexual symbols, male as well as female. Almost all contemporary Venetian bakers sell little phallic-shaped rolls which they pick from a big basket containing hundreds of them. These compact rolls with a hard, smooth, golden crust and a dense white texture (also found in Verona and Trieste), are called *pane piave, pane moro* (Moorish bread), or *massarine*. The Palace of the Dukes and the Museo Civico own several sixteenth-century paintings by such artists as Vicentino and Bassano, showing similar, sometimes biphallic or even double-biphallic breads.

Caen, in Normandy, was noted for little rolls with two side curls, similar to the Venetian ones, as well as brioches "with rounded heads on bulging bodies." Phallic-shaped breads were often made for weddings in several regions of Germany (Hamburg, Könisberg), while in France, comparable rolls were produced in Arles, in Aix-en-Provence, and in Italian bakeries in the old district of Nice. In Marseille, such breads are called *chichifregi*. On the Spanish as well as the French side of the Basque country, large loaves in the same shape are part of the baking repertory. An even more commonly held view is that the omnipresent classic Paris baguette is nothing more nor less than a phallic shape.

Female sexual symbols are not lacking in baking tradition. Many breads throughout French provinces are crown-shaped, like the *manchette,* which is slipped over the arm for carrying. Such a crown can be interpreted either as an echo of the Greek serpent biting its own tail (the crowns are often broken, with one end overlapping the other), or as a female sexual symbol. A number of painted decorations on Paris bakery windows at the end of the nineteenth century, representing a crown speared by a long loaf, would seem to lend some support to this theory.

Another undeniably feminine form, very widespread and ancient, is to be found in the long, almond-shaped bread, split lengthwise by a deep groove, which is sprinkled with manioc cassava flour just before baking so that it will not close up. These long loaves are widely available in Normandy (Honfleur, Bayeux), throughout the Southwest of France, and as far as Béziers and Montpellier, where they are called split breads *(pains fendus),* and are closely related to the female bread tradition of neighboring Spain: an elongated round loaf with rounded ends, split by a deep groove.

Many other rolls are also split, including the nineteenth-century *pistolet* still commonly found in Brussels. And some of these analogies have passed into various languages (such as the word *miche,* which is French slang for buttocks).

Sexual symbol breads:
male in Venice and Trieste,
female in Austria.

THE BAKER'S BREAD

As a major figure in the community, the baker has retained his legendary nature as he moves through history. Defiant at times when he has had to fight against industrial assaults, he (or she) continues to delight us with the most varied breads: baguettes, crowns, Provençal *fougasse*, Brittany's *crapelin*, Alsace's *subröt*, aromatic breads, German pumpernickel, and American corn bread.

With the revival of good wood-fire baked bread, traditional baking has adapted to the modern world. At the same time, bread is now eaten in all forms: sandwich, *pan bagnat*, *panini*, Monte Cristo, or hot dog and hamburger rolls. Both in the fabrication and in the consumption of bread, man's imagination appears to be limitless.

Left: **Wheat-flour dough left to rise in baskets.**

Opposite: **Baker at dawn. Photograph by J. Niepce, 1959.**

Pages 160–161: **Bakery and delivery of oven-baked bread. Anonymous eighteenth-century Venetian painting.**

Ano 1599 fu cosal de
Giacomo de Sabo
Auichario i sesio
fu restaurata
te Ani sy furidi

BAKERS

Parmentier, a devotee of good bread, and well-versed on the subject, had long ago considered and settled the question of how it could be obtained. In his *Avis aux bonnes ménagères sur la manière de faire le pain [Good Housekeepers' Advice on Breadmaking]* (1782), following a wealth of admonitions on the choice of flour, yeast preparation, kneading, and baking, he ended up recommending, in conclusion, that one should go and buy it at the bakery. "It will be much less troublesome to buy one's bread from the baker, who will always make it better and more cheaply than the thriftiest and most skilled of housekeepers."

The baker is unquestionably an irreplaceable presence in society, and as Marcel Pagnol has written, woe to the village whose baker has lost his wife.

It must be understood that a bakery is not like any other business. First of all, it's a place, an essential thread of the social and economic fabric of French life, of the originality of its culture, and of its joy of living. A good baker is sacrosanct. Without a baker, the soul of a town vanishes. No more meetings, no more early morning pleasures, no further zest for living, for existing in a humane world. The artisan baker gives us pleasure, satisfaction, and a focal point for social contact, just as much as he sells bread. If the baker departs, the loss is irreparable. An entire village can soon wither away, with yet another exodus of uprooted people toward the wasteful and polluting cities, and another step toward rural desertification. Some municipalities have resorted to subsidizing bakers so they will not leave, and so that the village may remain vital.

Good bread remains a yardstick of happiness, a symbol of the quality of life. It is a harbinger of our confidence in the future.

Bakeries Hot and Cold

While the number of artisan bakeries is dropping, the recruitment of bakery workers remains a problem in France. Young people recoil from work that starts at two o'clock in the morning, as well as from working on weekends and holidays.

Bakery customers are primarily urban, and they grow increasingly demanding as efforts are made to develop sales and satisfy their tastes. They expect a great variety of breads, of many forms and for every preference, and—above all—they always expect fresh bread. Otherwise, why had they abandoned the countryside and its stale, week-old bread!

It is rare for today's bakeries to sell only bread. Their survival has its price: they have become bakery-pastry shops, bakery-pastry-candy stores, or even bakery-pastry-grocery stores in villages where sales are slow. At that point, the shops often amount simply to bread outlets, "cold bakeries" as they are

Opposite: **Lionel Poilâne's old-fashioned loaves, in Paris.**

Below: **Eighteenth-century bakery sign. Male bread and New Year's pretzel, a female bread symbolizing life. Mezano, Italy.**

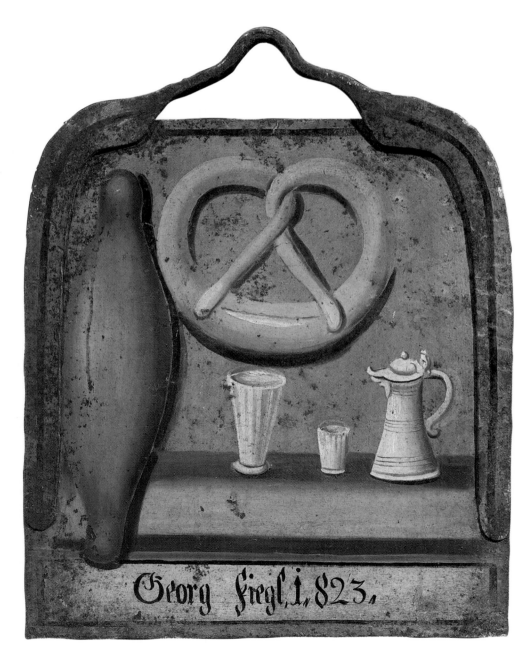

Georg Fiegl, i.823.

Kids in a Daze *(Les Effarés)*

Black against the fog and snow,
Against a grating all aglow,
Their asses spread,

Five kids—poor things!—squat and shake,
To watch a happy Baker bake
Hot golden bread.

They watch his white arms beat
The dough, and feel the heat
Of the bright stoves.

They hear the Baker softly hum
And hear a crackling sound come
From the baking loaves.

They are transfixed; they do not dare
Disturb the fragrant glowing air,
Warm as a mother's breast

For a rich man's holiday he bakes
Golden rolls and pies and cakes—
A sugary feast!

And then beneath the smoky roof
They hear a song from a savory loaf
— Just like a bird!

The warm window steams and glows,
And they squat in their ragged clothes,
Their senses blurred—

They even think that they're rich too—
Poor Baby Jesuses in a row
As the snow falls;

They stick their little noses in
Through the grating, moaning something
Through the holes

In a daze, saying prayers
And bending toward the lights
Of paradise,

So hard they split their pants,
And their shirttails dance
In a wind like ice.

Arthur Rimbaud

(From *Poems*, p. 18, translated by Paul Schmidt, Everyman's Library,
Pocket Poets, Alfred A. Knopf, New York, Toronto, English language
translation copyright © 1975 by Paul Schmidt, ISBN 0 679 43321 X.
Selection by Peter Washington first published in Everyman's Library
1994, Third Printing.)

Right: **Bakery interior.**
Anonymous nineteenth-
century Roman painting.

called, a phenomenon that is spreading in Germany and Switzerland, not to mention in the state-controlled countries where bread is produced exclusively by industrial bakeries.

In France, industrial bread production provides some 10,000 jobs in 350 baking centers, some of which can produce 2,500 baguettes an hour to supply the large supermarket chains. Some chains (such as Mie Câline, Point Chaud, Panichaude) bake at the point of sale, using frozen dough supplied by mass manufacturers. Industrial facilities produce 18% of the bread consumed in France, while the chain stores account for 7%, and these figures are climbing every year.

The Confédération Nationale de la Boulangerie (National Confederation of Bakeries), composed of artisan bakers who knead their own dough and bake it on their own premises, has long favored very specific legislation that would allow the consumer to easily distinguish a genuine artisan bakery from a simple frozen-dough baking facility.

The Raffarin decree of January 1, 1997, signed by the Minister of Commerce and Artisanship, restricted the term "baker" to *"exclusively those professionals who use selected flours to produce their own bread through its various stages: kneading, shaping of the dough, fermentation, and baking on the premises where the product is offered for sale to the end consumer."* But the Syndicat National des Industries de la Boulangerie et Pâtisserie (National Union of Bakery and Pastry Industries) appealed to the State Council, which annulled this decree in February 1998.

For their own protection, artisan bakers continued to clamor for a new state law or, at least, for formally accepted standards of quality. On April 3, 1998, the National Assembly finally adopted such a bill.

Right: **Early twentieth-century commercial bakery interior.**

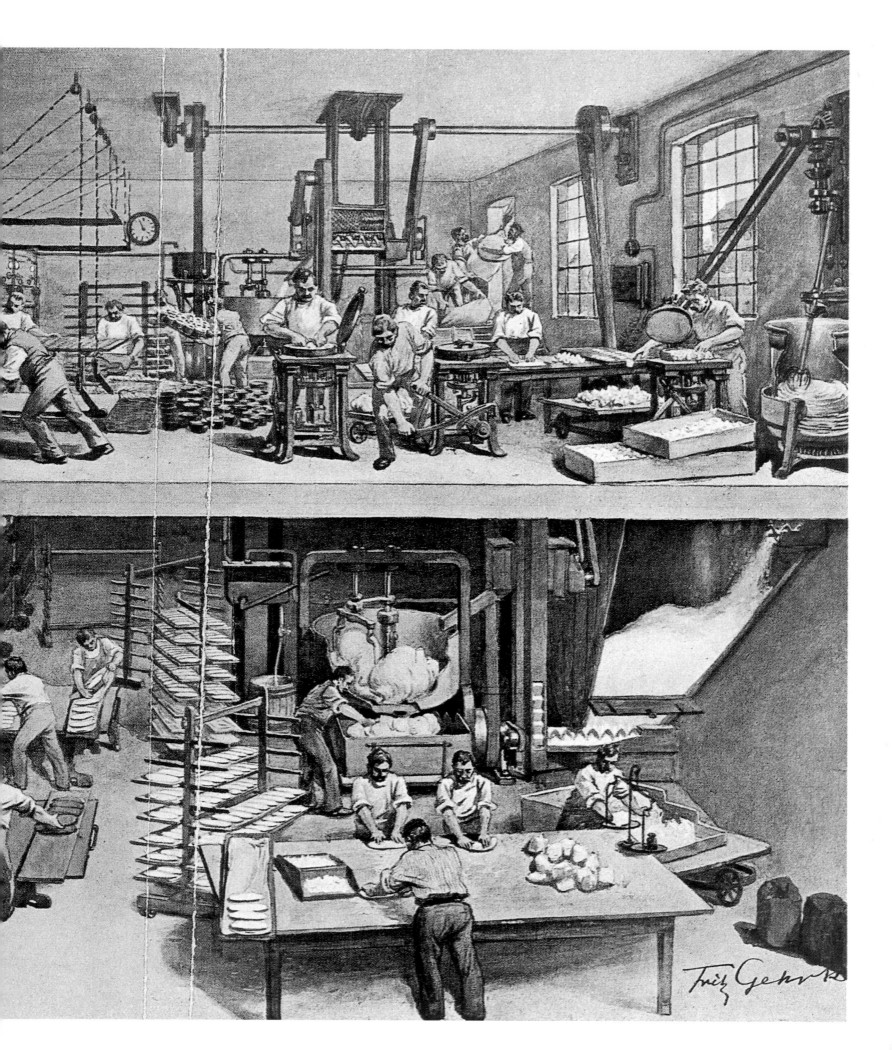

Bakers of Yesteryear

At the time of King Saint Louis, bakers were called *talemeliers,* and joining their guild involved a long process of initiation. After training successively as a winnower, sifter, kneader, doughman, or first assistant for five years, a young boy could then become an aspiring baker, and begin to work for himself. After buying a practice, he still had to complete a four-year "apprenticeship," during which he paid the King a weekly tax called a *tonlieu.* In addition, during the first year, he had to pay a fee of 25 deniers at Epiphany, 22 deniers at Easter, and 5 deniers and one obole at Saint-Jean. He kept his records on a staff, which the *coutumier* (forerunner of the tax collector) would notch at the beginning of each year, to show that the previous year's dues had been paid. Only then, could the aspiring baker finally call himself a master baker, provided always that he was a legitimate offspring, a subject of the King, a man of good repute, a member of the Catholic, Apostolic, and Roman Catholic faith, and free of any contagious disease.

Acceptance into the brotherhood of bakers was the occasion for a very curious ceremony. On the appointed day—usually the first Sunday in January—the candidate and the past masters of his community would come before the Grand Panetier, who was the King's officer in charge of bread and had jurisdiction over all the bakers of France. The applicant would present to this official an earthenware pot containing rosemary, sugared peas *(dragées),* walnuts, and *nieules* (a kind of rolled wafer), while saying: "Master, I have done and concluded my time, here is my pot full of nuts."

The Grand Panetier would then confirm with the tax collector, also present, the accuracy of this statement. Upon receiving an affirmative response, he would return the pot to the candidate and order him to smash it against the out- side wall of the house. With the completion of this gesture, the aspiring baker became a master.

All the bakers and their first assistants would then come in and the assembly would raise a toast to the prosperity of the young colleague. Each of them was required to attend these brotherly sessions under penalty of work interdiction for several days.

From a simple buffet, the acceptance reception soon grew into a full meal, which in turn became an elaborate banquet. This medieval ritual, whose spirit is reminiscent of the feudal vassal's tribute to his lord, gradually became obsolete with the passage of time. Toward the middle of the seventeenth century, it was replaced by the payment of a token gold coin, called an *hommage.* But the August 1711 Edict of Fontainebleau eliminated the office of Grand Panetier, and jurisdiction over bakers was transferred to the Police Lieutenant General.

This bill stated that the title of baker can be awarded exclusively to those professionals who personally perform "kneading, fermentation, and shaping of the dough, as well as bread baking" without recourse to the freezing process.

The Vogue for French Bread

Various events have been created recently to promote fine baker's breads and stem what statistics have documented as inevitable for years: the reduction in bread consumption. In 1992, Christian Vabret, Best Bakery Craftsman of France, created a Baker's World Cup, held every three years in Paris during Europain, the International Baking and Pastry Making Expo. Approximately ten countries take part in this team competition, which was won in 1996 by the French—living up to their reputation—and in 1999 by the team from the United States of America, thus confirming the tremendous advancements made in both the production and appreciation of good bread in America.

There is no doubt that the overall quality of French bread is recognized worldwide. Every baker who settles in New York, Montreal, Tokyo, or anywhere in South America to sell "genuine French bread" is said to prosper. China's first French bakery opened in Beijing in 1984, others followed quickly. The vogue for French bread has reached the Mahgreb, Africa, and even Pakistan, where Afghani bakers exiled because of the war have launched "French" bakeries and popularized "French" bread. In Bangkok, the Saigon Bakery sells French bread and a "French sandwich loaf" advertised as being prepared by the "Cordon Bleu de Paris." The "bread planet" continues to expand.

Below: **Itinerant French bread vendors in Laos.**

The Baker's Wife

(Marcel Pagnol, 1938)

THE FAMOUS ACTOR RAIMU HAS IMMORTALIZED THE
FIGURE OF THE ARTISAN BAKER. HIS WIFE HAVING LEFT HIM, HE
DESPAIRS AND UNINTENTIONALLY THREATENS HIS VILLAGE WITH
A TRAGIC BREAD SHORTAGE.

"If you just bring me back my Aurélie, then you'll have a
real baker. I will make you such bread . . . bread like you've never
seen. A bread so good that you won't use it just to go with something else; a bread that'll be a delight, a treat for gourmets. You
won't be able to say "I ate a cheese sandwich on bread," anymore.
You'll say "I ate a bread sandwich under some cheese." I'll make
ten pounds of bread everyday for the poor, and in every bread you
get, there will be a deep friendship and a big thank-you."

Leavenings and Yeasts

Fermentation is the very soul of bread. This is where bread gets its loft, its volume—that which communicates its flavor. By incorporating a fermentation agent into the dough when it is kneaded (brewer's yeast, starter, or industrial leavening), the baker triggers a complex and mysterious alchemical process. At a certain temperature (preferably around 68 to 77 degrees), the sugars contained in the dough are slowly converted into alcohol and carbon dioxide. This gas, seeking to escape, exerts pressure within the dough and makes it expand. The dough is then said to rise.

BREWER'S YEAST

The first yeast used by man was brewer's yeast, the foam that spontaneously forms on the surface of fermenting beer, from whence it is collected, washed in running water, and then dried. The Egyptians used it to make their bread. The Romans adopted it after having observed its use among the Germans and the Gauls. This yeast has the advantage of allowing fermentation at low temperatures, making it suitable for countries with cold winters. It was little used in medieval France, only re-emerging there in 1665 under the reign of Louis XIV, probably through the influence of Italian bakers, when they made *pain mollet,* which was prized for its lightness. But yeast was still being combined with leavening in order to comply with the Parliament's decree. After 1840, bakers from Vienna used it intensively in its pure state for their "poolish" fermentation. The first factory to produce this type of yeast was established at Maison-Alfort in 1872 by an Austrian businessman, Baron Fould Springer.

NATURAL STARTER FERMENTATION

Pain au levain, or naturally leavened bread, is synonymous with tradition and quality. There is quite an art to obtaining this sourdough, which serves as a fermentation agent. The first step in the procedure is called "mother starter," which is based on a simple flour paste (four pounds are enough) that is left to ferment for 72 hours; fruit is sometimes added to activate its fermentation, especially in winter (this can be grape must, apple, or the juice of one orange, which is the method used by the Moulin de la Vierge bakeries in Paris).

The baker then adds water and flour to this mother starter to "feed" it, as they say in the trade; two more fermentation cycles produce the "first starter," "second starter," and finally the "ready starter," which is used to start the dough for the daily batches, often amounting to several dozen pounds of bread. The volume of starter required is about one-third the amount of dough.

The baker need not repeat this complex operation daily. He can simply remove a little day-old starter, "fed" twice by adding water and flour to obtain the required amount of leavening. A batch of mother starter can easily live this way for a month. There are other, sometimes ancient, formulas for starter: in Greece, holiday bread is still kneaded with a leavening agent *(heptazymon),*

Left: **Baker's yeast.**

consisting of crushed chickpeas mixed with hot water and left to ferment seven times. In the United States and Canada, farmers used to make a dough starter left to ferment overnight with grated potato.

Most bakers have discarded natural leavening fermentation, since the processing takes a long time. Only a few—the best of them—still passionately cultivate this traditional method, particularly for making big, rustic, thickly crusted loaves of slightly sour bread. Bread made with natural starter is not as light and not as well risen as yeast-leavened bread, which is its virtue or its drawback, depending on an individual's preference.

BAKER'S YEAST

Since the 1920s, nearly all bakers have used only yeasts grown on molasses; this industrial yeast, composed of a live microscopic fungus of the species *Saccharomyces cerevisae,* is supplied in a dry, compressed form. The English, who prefer highly risen sandwich bread, add bicarbonate to the formula (in the nineteenth century it was ammonium bicarbonate).

Baker's yeast offers unquestionable advantages: it is more active and of even quality. Always ready and easy to use, it makes each batch autonomous and simplifies the baker's work, avoiding nighttime kneading chores. The yeast's drawbacks are also well known: while the forced rising to which it subjects the dough may please the consumer, the bread that results loses its flavor and freshness very quickly. This is why some bakers improve the bread's fermentation and its taste by adding a little dough taken from the previous batch, which has been allowed to ferment for three hours.

Modern yeast is nevertheless constantly being improved and the producers, who are often French (Société industrielle Lesaffre, in Marcq-en-Baroeul, is one of the world's leading manufacturers) are marketing increasingly pure yeasts with a better shelf life.

In kneading there is no geometry, no edges, no breaks. It is a seamless dream. It's work that can be done with the eyes closed. It is thus an intimate daydream. It also has a rhythm, a hard rhythm, a rhythm that takes over the whole body. It is thus vital. It has the essential characteristic of duration: rhythm.

What is more, this reverie bred by working the dough harmonizes perforce with the desire for a special power, with the male exultation of *penetrating* the substance, *stroking the inside* of substances, knowing the grain from within, mastering the earth as intimately as water masters it, reclaiming an elemental force, taking part in the struggle of the elements, of participating in an irresistible power of dissolution.

(Gaston Bachelard, *L'Eau et les rêves*
[Water and Dreams])

KNEADING, FLOOR TIME, AND OVEN LOADING

Considerations of leavening and yeast are only the beginning. The dough must be kneaded in a trough, which is now mainly a mechanical operation. The speed of various models varies, as does the motion of their metal beaters. But short, slow kneading is the golden rule observed by any good baker (if speed is set too high, the dough may become very white but its flavor will be lost). The dough undergoes an initial fermentation of about 40 minutes, called floor time; it is then fashioned into loaves of the desired shape, and allowed to rest and ferment for another three hours of finishing, during which the carbon dioxide develops, tripling the dough's initial volume by the end of the process. The final step is to score the top of the dough with the slashes that characterize French and Italian bread, among others, and facilitate the release of the gas in the oven, which must be loaded immediately after the second fermentation.

Opposite: **Kneading the dough into bread by hand.**

The Romance of the Parisian

This was in the early 1930s. Nameless at first, she was soon baptized "novelty bread." This is what Marcel Pagnol calls her in *The Baker's Wife*. But Provence, land of the *fougasse,* was not always this indulgent toward this Parisian, and Jean Giono did not look kindly upon what he called *"contemptible library paste which does not stick to your ribs."* Nevertheless, her charm eventually prevailed. Seduced, Doisneau and Willy Ronis photographed her countless times, carried in the arms of some mischievous Paris urchin, or of a man wearing a beret and a mustache, to the point of stereotype. Emboldened by her success and prestige, the city girl made converts. Imitations—often pale impersonations—and rivals were created, although one wonders why. Someone came up with a stubbier, you might say bastardized version, which has become the aptly named *bâtard.* Others, on the contrary, sought to make her smaller and leaner: this is how the *flûte* and its featherweight cousin, the slender *ficelle* came to be. But all this overlooked the fact that the baguette, 28 inches and ½ pound—an implausible length, an object of admiration and wonder for foreigners—remains inimitable.

Left: **Balthus,** *Le Passage du Commerce Saint-André,* 1952–54. Private collection.

THE
BAKER'S
BREAD

BREAD IN PARIS

"There is no better bread made anywhere than in Paris," wrote Louis-Sébastien Mercier in 1782. The bakers of Paris can trace their baking tradition back to the twelfth century, when the practitioners of the sifting trade bought the rights to their profession from the king and organized themselves into a guild. King Philippe Auguste (1180–1223) awarded a city-wide breadmaking monopoly to the sixty-two sifters of Paris. The word *bolengier* appears around that time, from the word *boulenc* in the dialect of Picardy, meaning "he who shapes the dough into a ball."

As was true of their Swiss and English counterparts, thirteenth-century Parisian bakers had to respect very specific rules concerning the quality, the weight, and the price of bread—rules that were enforced by regular militia inspections. The most valued kind of bread (the whitest bread even in those days) was the *pain de Chailly,* or *chaillé,* mentioned in a December 1372 ordinance, which was brought in from Chilly (now Chilly-Mazarin). Mentioned in the same ordinance was *pain coquillé,* which became *pain de ménage,* or *pain bourgeois;* and *pain bis, faitis,* or *de brode,* which contained more bran. Other breads in those times included *pain crémaillère,* or *pain-collier* shaped like a horse collar, which can still be found in the Dordogne and Charente-Maritime; and *pain-citrouille,* or pumpkin loaf, which was reputed to be very refreshing.

But French bread would not have established its enviable reputation without Italian influence. Two queens had a profound effect on French customs, replacing the heavy, thick, leavened but often badly risen loaf, made of coarse flour, with a lighter version: first, Queen Catherine de Médicis, wife of Henri II, followed by Marie de Médicis, daughter of the Grand Duke of Tuscany, who married Henri IV, King of France and Navarre, in 1600, and whose influence was even greater than that of Catherine. The Italian bakers she brought with her from Italy launched the fashion of *pain à la reine,* a luxury bread made of fine flour, which became *pain mollet* (or soft bread) in 1665, when

Les Halles retained its black airiness with its thousands of louvered light beams; people walked on the wide covered streets, while the distant halls remained deserted amid the swelling swarm of their sidewalks. At the Saint-Eustache corner, the bakers and wine merchants were taking down their shutters; the red shops, their gaslights lit, pierced the darkness along the gray houses. Florent was looking at a bakery on Rue Montorgueil, on the left, spilling over with the latest golden batch of bread, and he thought he could smell the comforting aroma of hot bread. It was four thirty.

(Emile Zola, *Le Ventre de Paris* [The Belly of Paris])

one of the bakers prepared it with brewer's yeast. This light-textured bread immediately became all the rage, but it also provoked a serious controversy about the dangers of the new recipe. On March 24, 1668, Louis XIV convened the doctors from the Faculty of Medicine to consider the potential harmfulness of using this yeast. Thirty of them, led by Claude Perrault, openly declared themselves *pain molliste,* "soft breadies" as they came to be called, in favor of the new soft bread. The forty-five other faculty members under Guy Patin issued an adverse opinion, saying that "the new yeast is harmful to health and damaging to the human body." A new committee was formed and, in a March 1670 decree, the Parliament at last authorized brewer's yeast on condition that it must always be used fresh and in conjunction with salt-rising yeast. This was a veritable slap in the face for the coarse-bread bakers, and in particular those from Gonesse, whose reputation had been excellent until then. But it was a windfall for the light-bread makers—in other words the majority of the Parisian bakers—and soft bread began to come into its own.

Opposite: **Early twentieth-century Paris bakery: basket with shoulder straps and wood cart for deliveries.**

Below: **Woman carrying bread. Paris, 1908.**

The surface of bread is marvelous first of all because of that near panoramic impression it makes: as if you had the Alps, the Taurus, or the Andes available at your fingertips.

An amorphous, belching mass was thus slipped for us into the stellar kiln where it hardened, taking on the shapes of valleys, crests, rolling hills, crevasses. . . . And all those flat surfaces, now so clearly defined, those slender slabs where light respectfully extinguishes its flames, without a thought for the unspeakable underlying weakness.

This lax and frigid underground that is the bread's interior has the flesh of sponges: its leaves or flowers are like Siamese sisters simultaneously joined at all their elbows. When the bread becomes stale, these flowers wither and shrink: they fall away from one another, and the body becomes brittle . . .

But let us break it: for bread must be less an object of respect than of consumption to our lips.

(Francis Ponge, *Le Parti pris des choses [The bias of matter]*)

According to Saint-Evremond (1614–1703), "it appeared successively under all forms and all characteristics: horned bread, Gentilly bread, *pain de condition, pain de Ségovie, pain d'esprit, pain à la mode, à la duchesse, à la maréchale,* and *à la Montauron,* named after the famous financier."

In the eighteenth century, the loaves, which had remained round until then, began to elongate and diversify. The Diderot and d'Alembert *Encyclopédie* describes no less than thirty variations in 1768. White bread made from white flour, *pain bis blanc,* or white whole wheat bread made from white flour and fine groats, and *pain bis* composed of a little white flour and bran flour, remain the most common types today. But there is also oat, barley, rye, corn (Turkish wheat), or buckwheat (black wheat). *Pain mollet* leavened with brewer's yeast is still made, along with *pain à la reine* made with a dough into which butter is incorporated.

At the end of the nineteenth century, the *Nouveau Larousse Illustré* still classified bread as white, whole wheat, black (from mixed buckwheat, rye, and wheat), and rye, according to the grade of flour used.

French taste underwent a second transformation with the arrival of Viennese bakers. The croissant, invented in Vienna in 1683, is introduced to Paris by Marie-Antoinette, "the Austrian," who marries the future King Louis XVI in 1770. The bakery at 12 rue Dauphine is the first to make these croissants in France. Beginning in 1840, Viennese bread became fashionable, i.e., bread leavened by a special technique called "poolish." Gradually, many bakery workers of Viennese origin helped to develop the production of "viennoiserie" or Viennese-style pastries.

At the same time, Parisian baking continued to diversify. The term *pain complet* was coined for "a bread whose ingredients include wheatmeal, *rebulet,* or fine bran." These late-nineteenth-century bakers made *pains ronds* (round breads), diagonally scored *pains longs* (long loaves), *pain fendu* scored very deeply lengthwise, *pain en couronne, pain de fantaisie,* or specialty bread, a long, thick *boulot,* and an oblong *pain polka* scored in a checkerboard pattern just before it went in the oven.

Bread Today

Today, the breads of Paris have changed again, and the large two or three kilo loaves of yesterday have practically disappeared. They have been lengthened to fit the canvas-covered woven baskets, *panetons* or *bannetons,* or the board and canvas *couches* on which the bread is laid for its second rising *(l'apprêt).*

The 500-gram bread is thick and oblong. The *bâtard* and *baguette* (the former specialty breads which have prevailed) are 70 cm long and 6 cm thick; both weigh 250 grams, but the baguette is longer. This Parisian baguette is made of white flour sifted at 75% so that it loses all but 25% of the wheat berry's minerals, and the dough is often over-kneaded, over-aerated—this excess air causes it to go stale rapidly. When the baguette is molded and cooked in its mold, the dough doesn't rise as well and the interior texture is denser.

Many bakers now offer specialty baguettes with dark, better balanced flour. The "Bannette" (registered trademark) uses a darker flour that has more flavor and keeps longer than the white baguette.

The *flûte* weighs 200 grams. The long, thin *ficelle,* which is half the weight and not quite the length of the baguette, and which was much prized for its crust, has virtually disappeared. The *couronne* (crown) and *pain rond* (round loaf) can hardly be found anymore except as new and more expensive "specialty breads."

The term *pain de campagne* (country loaf) covers many types of bread: it can mean no more than a plain bread dusted with flour for a rustic look and a higher price per kilo. Normally, it is made with what was still called "lesser quality flour" at the beginning of the twentieth century. The genuine or "traditional" country loaf is round, fairly large, and weighs from one to three kilos because the dough rises better when the volume is greater. The interior of this country bread is pale yellow, slightly tangy, and very flavorful. Ideally, it is kneaded slowly, with natural leavening, and

allowed more time to rise. It often contains 5 to 10% rye flour for stronger flavor and better keeping quality.

Pain complet, or wholegrain bread contains 90 to 95% of the berry's outer layers and other elements so that it retains vitamins (B1, B2, and K) as well as mineral salts (magnesium, calcium, potassium, and phosphorus). It is four times richer in these nutrients than white flour bread, and includes more fiber (9% of its weight) for better digestion. Its rich, dense dough satisfies hunger sooner and with less consumption. It remains fresh and flavorful for a week, and some consider it even more enjoyable when slightly stale. Whole wheat bread, sometimes called *tourte au levain,* is made with starter, or with a mixture of starter and baker's yeast. These breads used to be baked using an oak wood fire, which gave the loaf very good flavor, but this is rarely possible nowadays.

Rye bread must contain at least 60% rye flour. It has a strong flavor and is less digestible than white bread because of its higher cellulose content.

The flour for *pain au son* or bran bread has been only slightly sifted and retains the bran from the wheat's outer layers. The bread can also be made from white or whole wheat flour with the addition of powdered bran (5 to 20% of its weight).

In 1910, Apollinaire cited the various kinds of bread that Père Séraphin, the Archbishop's ordinary confessor, had imprudently blessed early in the morning in all the town's bakeries in the hope that "on that afternoon, the kingdom of god would arrive on earth." "There were long thin *flûtes,* and polka breads like round coins—golden from the crust, and silvered from the sprinkled flour—which had been kneaded by doughmen who knew nothing of heraldry; and there were little Viennese rolls like pale oranges, and household breads called *bouleau* or split breads, depending on how they looked."

(Guillaume Apollinaire, *L'Hérésiaque*)

Above: **Bread from the Valais region, marked with an iron stamp. Switzerland.**

Opposite: **Early twentieth-century bakery window in Paris.**

183

Since the bran content is not regulated, there are various grades or types of bran bread, moderate consumption of which is said to help digestion.

Pain biologique, or organic bread, uses flour from wheat grown without fertilizers, pesticides, or insecticides. The "organic" label is reserved for breads whose flour is of controlled origin.

Specialty Breads

Some bakeries still make a *baguette viennoise* from more expensive fine wheat flour milled from North African and American first-class wheat mixed with 4% powdered skim milk and malt extract (flour and germinated barley), plus sugar and shortening.

Pain de gruau can also be made from white flour enriched with groats (the part of the grain with the highest gluten content), as well as milk and malt.

Pain de mie (sandwich loaf) uses very white flour, is not very crusty, and is baked in a covered pan to attain its characteristic shape. This bread is high in calories; it contains milk, sugar, and shortening (3%), as well as additives to prevent molding and retard staleness (calcium propionate E282, ascorbic acid, and texturing agents). The English are fond of this type of bread, which they describe as "a sort of highly leavened bread obtained by adding ammonium bicarbonate to the dough." But is it reasonable to advertise a bread with a month-long shelf life?

Pain brioché, or brioche bread, contains even more calories (350 per 100 grams compared to 225 for white bread); it is enriched with sugar and eggs.

At the other end of the spectrum is unleavened bread, containing only flour and water, with no yeast, sugar, salt, or shortening. It keeps several months.

Right: **An assortment of French breads. On the left, the fougasse of the South. "Le Moulin de la Vierge" bakery, Paris.**

Right: **Molded bread with wheat grains,** *Körnlipicker.* **Basel, Switzerland.**

Below: **Deeply scored olive oil fougasse. Southern France and Italy.**

Right: **Poppy seed bagel.**

Left: **Olive bread.**

Right: **Raisin Brioche.**

Above: **Pepper rolls from Szechuan, with poppy seeds and fennel.**

Left: **Danish molded bread sprinkled with poppy seeds.**

The Baker's Horn

As surprising as it may seem, the image of a baker at his window, blowing his horn, was still familiar to citizens in the seventeenth century. It may have been the baker's signal that bread was ready for sale, or at least a way of communicating to his customers that his oven was hot, a reminder of the time-honored privilege he had to bake other people's bread. The forerunners of bakers, called *fourniers* (oven loaders), also had town criers running through the streets, loudly announcing and sometimes trumpeting that people could bring in their dough for baking.

This kind of setting seems unusual: no shop to enter, no counter, no shelves for stacking the bread. The bakery is still just a window giving out on the street—an *ouvroir,* or opening, as it used to be called—and the goods are displayed on a simple projecting wooden board, so that the buyer remains outside and the baker stays at the hearth.

Display or "window" breads *(pains de fenestre)* most aptly justify their name in this painting by Job Adriensz Berckheyde: this was the name of all novelty breads displayed in the baker's window as enticements and advertisements, in contrast to the common, or household bread. Here, pretzels, *cougnou, miches,* and little buns compete in beauty and allure under the longing gaze of the passerby, and they owe their forms entirely to the master baker's art.

Opposite: **Job Adriensz Berckheyde,**
The Baker's Horn, 1681. Ulm,
Deutsches Brotmuseum.

Picasso and the "Hand of Nice"

The South of France is famous for its *fougasse,* a flat elongated oval loaf with little leavening and a scored design in various shapes; these breads may be found as far away as Italy's Piedmont. They are sometimes sprinkled with sesame seeds, or with aniseeds colored yellow and blue, as in Monaco for New Year's and Easter. This ancient tradition dates back to the fifteenth century, when it was customary in some provinces to sprinkle crushed aniseed or marjoram on the table before setting out the shaped dough. One *fougasse* shape has evolved into a four-fingered hand known as *main de Nice,* or *pain Picasso,* named for the artist, and recorded in a famous Robert Doisneau photograph. Further north, *fouace* is a brioche bread kneaded with butter, sugar, and eggs.

The *fougasse* of Provence, the *souflâmes* of Charentes, and the *flambade* may contain olive oil. As for the *fougassette,* it is studded with diced bacon, while the *fibassier* of Cavaillon (Vaucluse) is a flat bread with bough-shaped cutouts.

The wheat flour and leavening *pain de Beaucaire* from the Rhône Valley is one of the best breads in France; in Montpellier, it is also called *pain à cornes* (known since 1372) because the dough is split lengthwise in the middle, with the edges of the split curled up like horns.

In the Drôme and as far as the Alpes de Haute-Provence, bakers still make *pognes,* bread crowns enriched with butter and eggs, which country people used to prepare for Easter, for the day of the Virgin Mary on August 15, and for the day of the patron saint of the village. These *pognes* were already being made in 1339, when the citizens of Valence would bring them to their baker for cooking. Lyon has its local crown and its breads with raisins, lard, bacon, or lemon, and the Alps their *pain bouli* (boiled). The *clouches* of the Landes are also boiled breads, as are the *miques* of Périgord, which are cooked in water, milk, and broth.

From the *Gascon Biphallique* to the Rodez *Échaudé*

In the Gironde, the *couronne bordelaise,* or Bordeaux crown, consists of eight or nine balls of dough forming a large ring; the tordu from Gers, Limousin, and Lozère is a closed twisted braid; Montpellier and Périgord have a very good, very crusty bread known as *pain de paillasse,* whose dough is wrapped in a towel and twisted both ways before baking. In the Basque country, in addition to the phallic-shaped bread (*gascon biphallique*) and corn bread (*méture,* yellow and compact inside), there is also a bread leavened only with fermented grape must. In the Pyrénées and in Alentejo, Portugal, or Salamanca in Spain, collections of carved wood bread stamps were used by each family to mark its bread before bringing it to the communal oven for baking.

Lionel Poilâne's 1981 *Guide de l'Amateur de Pain (The Bread Lover's Guide)* lists many more regional French breads, among them the Normandy festival *barret* bread, the *tourton* from Loire-Atlantique, and the *marquet,* which is soup bread in Mayenne; it continues with *pain miraud,* the *fouée* from Touraine, the rye *maniode* in Ardèche, the *charleston* of Aude and Hérault, the *pain coiffé* of the Eastern Pyrénées, the unleavened *échaudé* of Rodez, and the slowly fermented Corsican *coupiette.*

These breads, which embody the richness of local custom and culture, are endangered species, threatened not only by conformity and the standardization of eating habits, but also by the imperialism of the Parisian baguette.

Opposite: **Picasso with his** *fougasse* **hands. Photograph by Robert Doisneau.**

Below: **The** *fibassier,* **which is cooked in olive oil. Cavaillon, Vaucluse.**

The Thousand and One Names of *Pain Brié*

The dough of one bread in ancient Egypt was so tough that it could only be kneaded with the feet. The *blima* of Greece was also worked with the feet, just as were some of the compact, heavy bread discs that were found in Pompeii and are now displayed at the Naples Museum. This foot-kneaded bread was introduced to Normandy in the mid-fifteenth century, during the reign of Charles le Mauvais, King of Navarre, by a Spanish monk whose galleon had been shipwrecked. In 1567, in Paris, a baker from the Notre-Dame chapter introduced it successfully as *"pain de chapitre,"* or chapter bread. Later, in 1768, Diderot's Encyclopedia notes a *"pain chaland,"* "very white, made of crushed dough." Venice had little rolls baked from *pâte briée,* the *bussolai,* as early as the sixteenth century. In Algeria, this is called *pain espagnol,* or Spanish bread, since it was brought in by the Spanish. In Tunisia, it is known as *pain italien*—Italian bread—although no one remembers whether it came from the many Italians who used to live in that country, or was introduced through Algeria and Spain.

Depending on geography, this enigmatic bread called *"pain brié"* (from the verb *brier,* the Normandy form of *broyer* or crush, meaning "to knead the dough with a wooden roller"), took on various other names: *pain bordelais, pain de Dieppe, pain normand,* or *pain de port*—the latter called port bread because it is nourishing and sailors could keep it for a long time. It was also the bread eaten by the servants. On Normandy's farms in the 1870s, *pain brié* was baked just once a week in large 13 to 17 pound loaves, and was softened by dunking it into soup.

This bread has had many forms, suited to its many origins: round, semi-round, crown or almond shaped, or even formed into buns.

How can one recognize *pain brié*? It is compact, heavy, with a thick and barely cracked crust that is smooth and soft to the touch. The inside texture is tight, almost non-porous, and very white. Volume for volume, it is heavier than other types of bread. Because the dough contains only a minimum of water, so that it will remain compact, it requires long and arduous kneading. At one time, this was done by foot, but gradually, bakers began to use a *brie* or *brion,* a sort of long wooden rod. One man would gather up the dough under the rod and another would lower the rod, pressing down with all his strength to crush the dough. This kneading is now done in a trough, but still involves a manual technique. The dough must be as firm as possible, with a very low water content (35% to 40%), and consequently with a low yield of 265 pounds of bread for every 220 pounds of flour. The bread is still produced solely with salt-rising leavening. The oven is hotter than that used to bake a soft dough yeast-risen bread, and the baking takes longer—one hour for 6-pound loaves. All this preparation is time-consuming: one batch of *pain brié* takes six hours to prepare and bake.

Opposite: *Brié* bread.
Painting by Luis Eugenio Melendez (1716–1780).

THE RETURN OF GOOD BREAD

The sight of a line of customers waiting at a bakery is comforting and reassuring. Fortunately, there are still lovers of good bread, and bakers who love their profession, who respect the quality of the dough and its rhythms, as well as its pauses and its movements. When will we see the French counterpart of the coveted and privileged rank of "Living National Treasure" granted to Japanese masters of their crafts?

Flour mills, bakers, professional organizations, and bakery schools have been striving for the past twenty years to improve the quality of bread. Riding the current wave of renewed respect for nature, customers have also become increasingly demanding. They have learned, sometimes at their own expense, but also through numerous articles in newspapers and magazines, to recognize the difference between good bread and bread that is mediocre, dull, bland, and brittle, with no taste and no soul. Magazines and books devoted to food and good eating have been multiplying.

After a period of disenchantment with bread —when the French, better off and better fed, began to view it as bad and fattening—it is now recovering its role and regaining its prestige.

Good bread has made a tremendous comeback in recent years. It is no longer a basic survival food; and bakers have understood that they had to play the quality card to reverse the decline of bread consumption in the face of competition from more targeted and highly publicized products. Everybody responded: industrial bakers, by launching

Below: **Bread and milk are essential elements in many children's breakfasts.**

new quality products, and artisans, by diversifying their offerings and emphasizing quality.

All are alert to the new taste of the day—the concern with being authentic and natural (even if this "naturalness" is sometimes re-invented). The good bread of olden days for which we yearn may be somewhat mythical, a persistent dogmatic memory that we insist our modern city bakers restore to us. But no matter. The bakers are recapturing the gestures and fragrances of old-style bread, of tradition, of childhood. These breads are attractively presented, they smell good, they make you want to look, to touch, to bite into them.

At this point, all or nearly all flours are rich and varied, and the breads are usually good, even if one must sometimes forgo the overly standardized, classic Paris baguette, and venture to try the new options which recall the pleasures of yesteryear. More and more bakers are making delicious yeast breads, using wood fires, which remain tasty and flavorful for a week. These breads cost about the same by weight as Parisian baguettes (whether good or bad). Mandatory displays of prices per kilo simplify the comparison.

Bread-making artisans are regaining confidence. They are renovating their window displays, using color and materials that evoke natural themes. Bakeries are recovering their congeniality. Once again, buying bread has become one of life's repeatable pleasures.

Industrial bakeries have not been left behind. High-quality chain stores are multiplying: supermarkets such as Groupement Intermarché have rejected the tasteless, machine-processed and plastic-wrapped baguette in favor of point-of-sale baking centers. Some have even retained the services of genuine bakers who prepare and bake aromatic, premium breads (Auchan, Carrefour). As for the artisans, they are reviving regional bread, the vaunted "homemade" bread of the old days, made with leavening. (One of the bakers in Seilhac, in Corrèze, is offering flat delicious *tourtes* sprinkled with white flour, such as those once found throughout the Massif Central all the way to the Loire.) The best Auvergne food stores in Paris carry a variety of these breads, as well. In Vongnes,

in the Bugey (Ain), Alain Nambotin is baking big round leavened loaves in an old-fashioned arched oven fueled with firewood. Near Terrasson, René Neuville sells bread baked in his farm oven. And Christian Vabret, a baker in Aurillac, has established an advanced bakery training school.

The Regional Picardy Council has selected 300 bakers to revive the classic local bread made of 65% wheat flour with 35% spelt, an ancient rustic strain of wheat.

Above: **Café La Tartine, Rue de Rivoli, Paris.**

In Paris, Bernard Ganachaud (whose two daughters have opened a bakery in Vincennes), Michel Moisan, Jean-Luc Poujauran from the Southwest, and Lionel Poilâne from Normandy, are among the best known among the traditionalist bakers. Poilâne, in particular, has succeeded in making a famous name for himself throughout the world. He supplies cafés and restaurants, and is exporting to some fifteen countries including the United States, Japan, and Germany. His factory in Bièvres burns five tons of oak wood a day to fuel twenty-four ovens, supplies some six hundred sales locations, and employs about one hundred workers.

Many restaurateurs make a point of offering their customers a varied selection of carefully controlled quality bread, and some of them—such as Jean-Claude Ferrero, Gaston Lenôtre, Michel Moisan, Alain Passard, Alain Raichon, and Joel Robuchon—bake their own.

Some creative bakers are also finding ways to make their bread tempting to buy through the

use of innovative shapes. One trend is toward animal loaves: crocodiles, turtles, sometimes snails and frogs. But there are also elaborately decorated festive specialty breads which look marvelous when set before the guests.

This infatuation with old-fashioned bread can even inspire vocations based on the simple life. For certain city people moving to the country, the presence of an old bread oven on a farm can mean the opportunity to bake homemade bread from stone-ground flour. Ecological brochures and manuals offer countless recipes for making your own bread—without any guarantees of success. It is sometimes wise to find associates. The citizens of Guyencourt-sur-Noye, in Picardy, have decided to bake bread as a joint activity during village celebrations. After all, domestic bread-baking used to be one of the essential rituals in rural communities.

Finally, the media should be given due credit for contributing—in no small degree—to this return of good bread. Advertising agencies have come up with all sorts of slogans in magazines and on television, to evoke the concept of nature and quality, associating bread directly or indirectly with cheese, wine, farmers, monks, and the bounty of the soil in general. There was also a memorably successful television series on master bread craftsmen *(Maîtres du Pain)*. Beautiful loaves of bread have been featured in various fashion magazines, as symbols of rustic elegance and discretion. But one of the best slogans is the one that the Bakers' Union has used on its posters: "The French make the best bread."

Opposite: **Bakery at the Ecomuseum in Ungersheim, Alsace.**

Right: *Couque* **from Dinant, Belgium.**

BREADS OF THE WORLD

An invitation to sample the breads of the world involves an extraordinary voyage. A trip through space of course, the physical space of soils and climates: to the North, toward the cold, where wheat growth ends, but where the world of rye and of black bread begins, this same black bread that is disdained in the Mediterranean countries, home of wheat and white bread. Geography imposes its own conditions: mountain people do not make the same bread as the people of the flatlands.

It is also a trip through time: each bread has its history, the history of a village, of a community. Bread-making transmits different forms of expertise, and symbolizes cultural identity: in Switzerland, for instance, each canton has a specific bread that has its own shape, its own baking technique, and its own flavor. The bakers of the Valais often decorate their breads with a city's coat of arms. A loaf of bread can also bear witness to an uprooting, or a culture shock, sometimes in a very literal sense, like the pioneer bread produced by the people who set out to conquer the New World. Bread can also reflect the fads and fashions adopted by a society: Japan, which was once totally or almost totally unaware of bread, is now living on Paris baguette time, together with a few other examples of the French baking art. Certain breads may refer directly to some historical anecdote, such as the Viennese bakers' *hörnchen,* the little horn-shaped ancestor of the croissant that celebrated Vienna's victory over the Turkish forces.

Bread resembles the bread-maker. Is it any wonder then, that there is such an incredible diversity of breads offered by bakers everywhere in the world?

Left: **French bread in Tunisia.**

Opposite: **Itinerant vendor of French-style bread. Hanoi, Vietnam.**

Pages 202–203: **Flatbreads at the Kachgar market in Chinese Turkestan.**

BREADS OF EUROPE

Belgium and Its Pistols

Belgium has benefited both from the white bread traditions of the Mediterranean and from the more Germanic influences of whole wheat and whole grain bread.

The famous *pistolet* of Brussels is a small, round, split, milk roll served on Sunday morning. Another bakery specialty, the *cramique,* is traditionally eaten as a Sunday afternoon snack. It is a whole wheat raisin bread that is served in slices. *Nic-nacs* are bread alphabets with a pink or blue sugar glaze, sold by the bagful. The *épi* baguette is very common, and some bakery-pastry shops are starting to sell animal-shaped breads. Braided and cumin-seeded loaves are popular in Jewish neighborhoods.

In Verviers, the *craquelin* replaces the *cramique.* The delicious shortbread cookies called *speculoos* are available year-round, along with *main d'Anvers,* an aniseed gingerbread, Verviers marzipan, and the multi-shaped *couques* of Dinant. Bruges is particularly famous for its biscuits.

The White Bread of Italy

The Italians, custodians of the secrets of Greek bread as transmitted through ancient Rome, disseminated the taste for white bread in Europe. In 1533, Catherine de Médicis brought Italian cooks with her to the French court, where they exerted a significant influence on French taste: they practiced a lighter style of cooking, developing the use of bread, and introducing pastries and elaborately prepared dishes. Marie de Médicis reinforced the Italian influence throughout the kingdom: pasta made from Italy's hard wheat was already known in the Middle Ages, and Italy has preserved its baking traditions ever since, despite the drawbacks of large-scale industrialization.

Among the countless regional breads is the

Opposite: **Household bread in Tuscany, Italy.**

Below: *Pistolets,* **slit, feminine Sunday rolls. Brussels, Belgium.**

Above: **Bread delivery in
Desulo, Sardinia, Italy.**

ciabatta, a Northern Italian loaf created somewhere near Como. Not only the Italians, but also
the British appreciate its inner texture, which becomes almost cake-like from olive oil, and its tender, flavorful crust; the *biova,* a cylindrical, thick-
crusted bread originating in Turin; and *grissini,*
the fine, crisp breadsticks made from wheat flour
and olive oil, originally from Piedmont, but found
everywhere today throughout the Italian penin-
sula. They are a welcome treat served with drinks
before a meal, although, unfortunately, they are
usually factory-made.

The *fruste ostinchi* of Tuscany is a hard
wheat bread, while the *pagnotta* is a plump round
loaf made mostly of whole wheat flour. The *pia-
dina* of Romagna is kneaded with milk, placed in
an iron pan, and turned over to bake on both
sides; two of them are used to make a traditional
ham sandwich eaten with a salad. *Focaccia,* Italy's
version of *fougasse,* is also among its major
achievements. It is often garnished with fine herbs,
rosemary, onion, cheese, and so on.

The Neapolitan *cafone* is very white, which
accounts for its good reputation. *Pane de Trani* is
a hard wheat round loaf (made with the same
durum wheat as that used in pasta), from the
Apulia region, which also features *pan pugliese,* a
savory country bread owing its tender texture to
olive oil and its flavor to *biga* (an Italian leavening
agent left to mature for at least twelve hours).

Italy has hundreds of other regional breads
to offer, like the *ciriola* which the Romans adore,
the Lombardy region's *francesina* that resembles
the French *ficelle,* or the unsalted wheat bread, *pan
scapio,* from Tuscany, where it is extremely popular.

Frascati, forty kilometers from Rome, is an
important production center for sugared breads
shaped like people or animals, trees or flowers,
devils and monsters. Sicily and Sardinia offer very
beautiful white holiday breads sculpted into spirals, animals, or flowers.

Calabria has successfully maintained both the
Gerocarne village tradition of homemade gingerbreads and the ex-voto offerings handcrafted by
Soriano pastry makers. In former times, these were
probably made from fruits preserved in grape must.

Left: **Leavened bread.
Switzerland.**

Pages 208–209: **Baker's
display in Cairo, Egypt.**

Italian and international tourism has not reduced the demand for all these specialties, and those who provide them can make a very comfortable living.

Switzerland: A Confederation of Breads

Switzerland, with its mixture of flatland farmers and individualistic mountain people, offers a great variety of breads. There are about two hundred types—almost as many as in Germany— available from the 4,500 artisan bakeries that bake 600 tons of bread daily. Each canton has its own specialties, and the simplest town bakery may offer up to fifteen different choices, varying in form, size, flour composition (white bread, semi-white, black), and hydration ratio, meaning the amount of water added to the dough.

The variety of rye breads in Switzerland is notable. They include pure rye, or rye mixed with several other grains, such as the *apfelnussbrot* combining rye, wheat, barley, spelt, and millet, or the peasant bread which is a mixture of two-thirds wheat and one-third rye. The flour used in the rye

crown generally contains two-thirds rye and one-third wheat. This bread is shaped into a ring that can be stacked on posts or bread racks. Sometimes, the dough is sprinkled with cumin seed.

The *pain de seigle valaisan* is a large, round, fairly flat loaf of pure rye flour and leavening. Its surface is floured before baking, and the top is very crusty; it is sometimes studded with walnuts. This is mountain bread, the kind that keeps for a long time, all winter long. Bakers in the Valais decorate these loaves with additional designs in relief, or by stamping the shaped dough (before resting and baking) with an iron that represents flowers, initials, a shield, or the town's coat of arms. These breads are sold in every Valais bakery and as far as Basel, in bakeries or health food stores.

The most commonly found bread in the Helvetian Confederation is *pain bernois*. It is a semi-white, round loaf deeply scored across its surface. *Pain lucernois* is a whole wheat or semi-white oval, similarly scored lengthwise, and often still made with leavening. It is always baked to a deep brown color, in two-kilo, one-kilo, and one pound sizes.

Ex-votos and The Pilgrimages of Calabria

In Italy's Calabria, the provinces of Reggio and Catanzaro have established a significant tradition of hand-shaped gingerbreads, the *mustazzuoli*. These breads serve as ex-votos *(voti)* and as pilgrimage or festival mementos called *scherzi* (amusements) which have endless variations limited only by the imagination of the pastry maker *(mustazzuolaro)*.

The ex-votos are a specialty made by the bakers of Soriano for the local pilgrimages on the Sunday after August 16 in honor of Saint-Roch, patron saint of various neighboring villages. (This saint, born in Montpellier around 1295, is also invoked in France for protection against contagious diseases, and once upon a time, against the plague.) The offerings represent the various parts of the body that may be afflicted, or the family seeking protection.

They are offered by penitents, usually people from the village or its surroundings, during a procession along the main streets after Sunday Mass. The petitioner attaches a silver offering to a sort of beribboned banner held by a festival committee member leading the procession; he then approaches the statue of the saint and rubs his ex-voto against the figure or its pedestal, depending on how high he can reach. Then, as the procession moves along, the offering is placed in a large basket carried by another member of the Festival Committee.

The following morning (after the saint has been returned to his church), the ex-votos are auctioned off on the plaza outside the church.

The sale is held by the Committee which uses the proceeds for its activities: organizing the festival, and providing hospitality and payment to the musicians hired for the procession. Singers, comic entertainers, little troupes of actors, and the inevitable majorettes must also be engaged for the evening's festivities. And lastly, expenses and fees must be paid to the fireworks crews in charge of setting off the firecrackers and noisemakers that announce the festival that morning, and for the fireworks that night.

Left: **Ex-votos are offered by penitents during the Saint Roch pilgrimage for curing illness, on the first Sunday after August 16. Soriano, Calabria, Italy.**

Below: **Saint Roch ex-voto showing the part of the body to be healed or the family to be protected. Soriano, Calabria, Italy.**

Pain saint-gallois consists of four balls of dough joined together into a round loaf that can weigh up to five pounds. *Pain vaudois* is semi-white, fairly soft textured, and scored with a deep cross. The elongated *pain bâlois* is made from highly hydrated dough that is rolled in flour before baking.

The bread of Italian-speaking Switzerland is ultra-white (made with very fine flour and oil), and is kneaded for a long time to incorporate a great deal of air. *Pain tessinois* is shaped from five or six small oblong pieces of dough joined lengthwise, and broken off into rolls for serving. The dough for *pain milanais* is flattened, rolled up, and cut in two.

But in Switzerland, as elsewhere, the tendency to eat bread made exclusively of white flour has begun to wane in favor of darker, more complex, and better balanced breads.

The Land of Black Bread

As in Russia, rye breads, black breads, have been the breads of choice in Germany, but Germans have also demonstrated their appreciation of other whole grain breads, which derive the full benefit of the grains, including the husks, those husks which white-bread-oriented Mediterranean countries often hold in contempt.

As in France and Switzerland, it was the monks in Germany who were the first to bake bread on a large scale. The first bakers' guilds were organized in the tenth century, exercising strict control over bread quality as well as apprentice training. The present-day Guild of German Bakers lists two to three hundred types of bread for the most varied dishes and meals. The Central Bakers' Association employs three full-time inspectors to taste the breads produced by their members, and 85% of German breads are rated "good" or "very good" by the Institute of Baking Sciences.

German rye breads are consistently excellent and their importance and variety have not diminished. Each region has its traditions and its favorites, such as *holzlucken, urtyp,* and *buckeburger,* among many other breads of rye flour alone, or those mixed with different proportions of wheat flour, whether coated or not with seeds and flour.

It is also in this country that major produc-

ers of hermetically sealed sliced rye bread first established themselves. One of the most famous of these specialties is *pumpernickel,* the leavened black Westphalian bread made of pure rye flour, vegetable oil, water, and salt. Legend has it that, during one of his German campaigns, Napoleon was served a local bread which he found coarse, being made of whole, unmilled rye grain. He sniffed it and declared it "good enough for Nickel," his horse. The words "bon pour nickel," mispronounced with the German accent, became the name "pumpernickel."

Wheat and rye are now widely used, as well as other grain mixtures with various grades of milling and flour extraction rates, to make bread baked with natural or chemical leavening agents.

Bread lovers in Northern Germany prefer brown or dark whole grain bread, while those in the Southern Länder, closer to Italy, are more interested in the whiter varieties.

Each region has its typical shapes—in Westphalia, Berlin, Bavaria, and so on. In the Black For-

Above: **Raisin Danish, apple turnovers, brioche, and croissants.**

est region, snowbound in winter, breads tend to be large: the big elongated loaf called *Schwartzwalder Bauerbrot* (Black Forest peasant bread) weighs three kilos and the *Schzütier Volkorn Flinbrot* is a long one-kilo loaf decorated with dots and lines. One baker is even providing the citizens of Feudenstadt with a *Pariser langbrot,* a "long Parisian bread" weighing 500 grams. Elsewhere in Germany, many different kinds of poppy seed, pepper, or onion-stuffed breads are much appreciated.

Viennese Baking

The typical French breakfast croissant actually came from Austria under the name *hörnchen,* or little horn. When Vienna was besieged by the Turks in 1683, it was the bakers who sounded the alarm in the silence of the night, when they heard the Turks digging underground as they tried to reach the central powder and munitions depot. These Viennese bakers, who already enjoyed an excellent reputation, were rewarded by the Hapsburgs, who granted them the privilege of making little rolls in the shape of the crescent moon on the enemy's banners.

The first Viennese pastry shop was opened in Paris in 1789, at 12 Rue Dauphine, by a pastry-maker in the service of Marie-Antoinette, wife of Louis XVI. Then, in 1837, a certain August Zang arrived from Vienna with recipes for Austrian breads, which were still unknown in France at that time. In 1840, he opened a "Viennese bakery" on the Rue de Richelieu, and its tremendous success quickly inspired others throughout Paris. His secret was a so-called *poolish* or Polish-style yeast which was actually discovered in Vienna, and which made the dough rise faster, without the sour taste that leavened bread can acquire if its fermentation is not properly supervised.

The reputation of these breads from Vienna, seat of the Austro-Hungarian Empire, was enhanced even further with the adoption of the first Hungarian steam-driven roller mills, which yielded high quality flour (this is the system that the Americans later adopted for their industrial flour mills). This technique preserves the berry's gluten-rich coating, while eliminating its bran.

Thanks to the 1878 and 1889 International Expositions, Parisians had a chance to taste these fine wheaten breads. In 1895, a French flour mill began to use the Hungarian process, which was later adopted by the Grands Moulins de Paris, as well. Since then, Viennese bread has been synonymous with quality and, until recently, many a Paris bakery advertised the magical formula "Viennese Bakery" in gold letters on its glass storefront.

Scandinavian Bread

In the cold climates of Northern countries such as Sweden or Finland, the traditional bread is rye, *tunnbröd,* baked in thin round sheets hung on ceiling rods—as a precaution against rodents—and kept all winter.

The ever-present black bread is sometimes filled with lard and fish, or garnished with sesame and poppy seeds, as in Denmark. For Christmas and Saint Lucia's Day, specially decorated breads are still baked at home. In Finland, at Easter, people prepare a rye flour cake flavored with malt, molasses, and bitter orange rind.

Another Nordic specialty is *knäckerbröd,* a sort of flat, unfermented rye and wheat biscuit, which is commercially made and distributed worldwide.

Great Britain and Its Traditions

Wheat bread is a relative late-comer to the United Kingdom. Previously, rye and oats were the more common crops, particularly in the cold climate of Scotland and Ireland. Thus, *bannock* is used to designate all sorts of unleavened flat breads, often made of barley, from those regions (as well as from Northern England), which are not well suited to grain cultivation. The contemporary pudding is a descendant of ancient flour and suet dishes or minted meat stews.

Below: **Croissants appeared in Austria during the 1683 siege of Vienna by the Turks.**

Gingerbread

Europe discovered gingerbread thanks to the Crusades. The Germans seem to have been among the first to make this yeast cake in imitation of the *panes mellitos* (honey bread), brought back from Jerusalem. The spice-merchants of Nuremberg were already supplying bread to the Basel City Council in 1370. In France, gingerbread was introduced by Philippe le Bon, Duke of Burgundy, who discovered it in Courtrai, Flanders, in 1452, and liked it so much that he brought some artisans back with him to France. Reims and Strasbourg were the first cities to produce gingerbread, and it soon became a famous specialty.

In those days, gingerbread was the prerogative of princely and aristocratic tables, and the royal courts of Charles VII, François I, and Louis XIII, were said to prize it. It contained honey, of course, but tasted quite different from our own because it was also highly spiced with cinnamon, ginger, pepper, clove, anise, cumin, fennel, and coriander. The pepper gradually disappeared from the recipes as sugar came into use beginning in the seventeenth century. England is now the only country to still make a highly spiced, not very sweet gingerbread.

The gingerbread dough of former times was packed into hollowed out wooden molds for baking. The molds were elaborately decorated in remarkably fine detail, representing ladies in fashionable dress, princes or lords in full regalia, knights, harnessed carriages, and footmen in livery—in other words the whole courtly society.

Above: **Birthday gingerbread man. Amsterdam, Netherlands.**

In France, Dijon has come to be the main competitor of Reims. Its gingerbread is made from wheat flour, unlike that from Reims, which mixes rye flour, lemon peel, anise, and spices. The cities of Montbéliard and Metz also eventually developed a gingerbread tradition of their own.

THE FOIRE DU TRÔNE AND ITS PIGS

In the eighteenth century, a golden era of gingerbread, the rise of a new urban middle-class clientele compelled gingerbread bakers to modify their decorations. City life took center stage, with portraits of ladies, bourgeois, soldiers, and city coats of arms. Religious subjects also multiplied, from Adam and Eve, the Madonna and the Christ Child, to the Three Kings, the Crucifixion, and even angels.

These elaborate gingerbreads, too beautiful (and too hard) to be eaten, were really intended to serve as decorations. Other, plainer, softer, and eventually sweeter ones, became standard treats at country fairs. In Paris, the Gingerbread Fair, which would later become the Foire du Trône, was held at Easter within the precinct of the Saint-Antoine Royal Abbey. The fair's celebrated gingerbread pigs, which are still the trademark of the event, date back to 1719, when the king had forbidden the monks to bring their pigs to the fair. To avenge themselves, the monks got the twenty-odd gingerbread makers who took part in the event to sell a multitude of little gingerbread pigs.

Right: **Gingerbread, offered by young men to their fiancées. Hand-colored wood engraving. Alsace, c. 1850.**

Below: **Old advertisement for honey gingerbread using a traditional Flemish recipe.**

WAGNER, GINGERBREAD STYLE

In the nineteenth century, traditional gingerbread decorations were abandoned and subjects became simpler. They began to refer to current events, and numerous political or satirical allusions to Napoleon, Charles X, Bolívar, General Boulanger, Garibaldi, and so on, made their appearance. Bakers drew inspiration from the fashion of the moment and their production bore witness to its whims. As the popularity of gingerbread grew, the great classic tradition was extinguished by the customers' changing tastes and by mass production. The early nineteenth century saw the advent of gingerbread cookie-cutters manufactured first in Hamburg, then in Paris beginning in 1832. From that time on, production methods were turned around: the dough was no longer fitted to the mold and imprinted with all its details; instead, the cutter stamped out a mere outline shape from a sheet of dough. The forms inevitably became standardized and the decoration could only be a surface adjunct traced with sugar after baking.

The emerging tourist industry has encouraged all sorts of geographic or cultural clichés. The specialty of Bayreuth is now gingerbread decorated with the main themes of Wagner's Cycle and packed in a tin featuring the composer's portrait.

In a few contemporary cities, such as Vienna, Aix-la-Chapelle, or Torun in Poland, bakers still adhere to the time-honored molded forms; but the gingerbread, rather than being the original article, is really *printen,* made of harder dough which is closer to a biscuit. In Zurich, the *Züri-Tirgel,* a very hard anise bread, is still shaped in wooden molds with traditional or religious decorations. These confections are kept one year before being eaten.

The *couques* of Dinant, Belgium, are probably the closest evocation of the incredible products of yesteryear. The V. Collard factory, in particular, is one of the oldest established European gingerbread concerns. Here again, however, the works are more appropriately admired than eaten. In addition to His Majesty the King, subjects include landscapes, Saint-Nicholas rescuing little children, lovers' hearts, goddesses and harvesters, fruits, baskets of flowers and vegetables, and numerous animals: elephants, snakes, horses, lambs, pigs, rabbits, fish, or cats. At the Foire du Trône, displaced for one more year to the Reuilly lawn at the edge of the Vincennes woods, the little traditional pigs are still for sale. As a rule, they may be neither very good tasting nor in very good taste, but surrounded by delighted children, the seller will "baptize" each purchase with the name of the individual child in colored sugar.

Opposite: **Gingerbread.**

Above: **Bread deliveryman
in England.**

The taste for white bread is thus comparatively new. From breakfast to dinner, for toast or sandwiches, the sandwich loaf remains the inescapable specialty of British baking. Nevertheless, Great Britain is not devoid of baking traditions, such as saffron bread from Cornwall (one of the regions where crocus was cultivated and used). The various English gingerbreads have also retained their traditional flavors of spice, honey, anise, cinnamon, clove, cardamom, cumin, or nutmeg. In Scotland, bakeries make morning rolls called *baps*, glazed with milk and generously dusted with flour before baking, according to Scottish custom. These tender, light-textured buns or rolls, as they are called elsewhere, are equally good with savory or sweet dishes.

The Irish are partial to a traditional soda bread that is not made with yeast but with bicarbonate of soda instead. This is a whole wheat bread, which also contains buttermilk or even yogurt, and may include raisins, currants, and so on. It was once baked in a kettle with embers covering the lid.

Finally, the tradition of harvest loaves, the famous English sculpted breads, has not completely disappeared, since a London baker has decided to revive it. This bread is over sixty centimeters high and forms a great sheaf of some hundred stalks of wheat spread out in a circle.

The Yellow Breads of Portugal

In Portugal, corn bread or *broa de milho* remains as important as ever. This traditional peasant bread, which was still cooked on the farm not so long ago, is now sold in many of the country's bakeries. It is nourishing, with a beautiful inside color ranging from pale to pronounced yellow, depending on the quality of the corn and the amount of wheat mixed into it. It is traditionally served with stews and soups such as the *caldo verde* (cabbage soup).

Braided Breads

Braided bread, made of wheat flour and nearly always decorated, belongs to the same cultural dimension as rye bread: it is found mainly in Russia, in Northern countries, and in Central Europe. It is hand-braided by the housewife or the baker from two long rolls of dough; it is an endless bread that symbolizes life.

This bread still exists in Russia, and the pastry shop across from Saint-Alexander-Nevski Cathedral, in Paris, on Rue Daru, sells many of them on Sunday mornings after church services. Braided breads are also very common in Germany and Central Europe, where they are a holiday tradition of long standing for Eastern Jews: all Jewish bakeries carry *challah,* sometimes containing raisins, and reserved for the Sabbath meal. By way of Germany, braided bread reached Alsace and Savoie under the name of *tresse savoyarde* (Savoie braid), and came to Switzerland as *tresse,* considered the perfect Sunday morning bread. Italy and the Balkans have also adopted it as an Easter bread, often containing a red-dyed egg within its twists, as a symbol of fertility, life, and rebirth.

Always made with wheat flour, braided bread has gradually been enriched with milk and eggs to become a braided egg bread. In addition, braided loaves are frequently sprinkled with seeds, another ingredient of abundance and happiness. According to a German tradition adopted by the Jews, poppy seed is used most often, adding its flavor to the beauty of the braided bread.

Below: **Braided bread symbolizing life. Easter bread from Yugoslavia.**

BREAD MADE IN THE U.S.A.

The United States is presently the largest wheat producer, accounting for more than one-seventh of world crops, but this has not always been the case. The food plant native to America is corn, the grain which Christopher Columbus called "Indian wheat," and which the first pioneers ate, as did the Indians before them.

The first European immigrants to land in the New World on the *Mayflower* in 1620 survived only thanks to corn cultivation. They also sowed rye and wheat brought from Holland. The rye adapted well, but wheat did not, so that the bread eaten by the immigrants was often made from mixed corn, rye, and wheat flour.

The Pioneer Spirit

Since the myth of the pioneer spirit is still very much alive in the United States, it is not surprising that corn bread, corn pancakes, and corn muffins are still so frequently made by American housewives and enjoyed at coffee shops, diners, and from street-food vendors. The batter is sometimes made of pure meal, such as the corn pone of Indian origin, but as in the case of the classic corn bread, it is most often mixed with wheat flour so that the loaf will rise better, since corn meal has no gluten. Corn bread has a naturally sweet flavor, and as a result, Americans often prepare it with milk, sugar, and eggs (a special version is Southern spoon bread —a soft bread made of cornmeal mixed with milk, eggs, and shortening that is served with a spoon).

Corn recipes in the United States vary greatly, depending on the region. In the Midwest, it is boiled, served with grated cheese and tomato sauce, grilled or fried meat, and vegetables. The dough is often fried on both sides in a skillet, served with fresh or processed meat, fish, or vegetables, or else covered with molasses.

Above: **Bread delivered by horse-drawn carriage in the United States in 1890.**

Baking One's Own Bread in Vermont

Many individuals in the United States, rejecting the idea of anonymous and tasteless bread, have turned to baking their own. "Why not try to do it yourself," they ask themselves. "It will be better, more enjoyable. It will bypass shipping and marketing costs and it will save energy."

Jules and Hélène Rabin have built their own oven, a few yards from their house in Vermont: a single compartment of refractory bricks built into a dome and covered with a thick layer of sand to conserve heat. The oven is filled in the morning with scrap wood from the nearby lumber mill. After heating for eight hours, it is cleared of embers and ashes, cleaned, and humidified. There is enough stored heat for six hours of baking for the loaves set directly on the flat brick hearth.

The dough must be prepared in the morning by adding to the water, flour, and salt, some natural starter made the night before. The dough is kneaded in a mechanical mixer, in 60-pound batches, and allowed to rise until mid-day. Early in the afternoon, it is divided and shaped into round loaves (or long ones for French bread), and left to rest so that it may rise a second time.

These two people produce about 200 breads of four different types on each of three baking days, for a daily total of 240 pounds.

Jules and Hélène Rabin do not want to increase their output, in spite of the growing demand from neighbors, private customers, stores, and restaurants, so that they can still have time for other activities and can continue to take pleasure in the baking to which they devote 3 ten- to twelve-hour days each week.

They deliver their bread throughout the neighborhood, where everybody knows them. Their avocation is an opportunity for them to cultivate valuable social relations. Above all, they say, their activity motivates people to talk and meet, and contributes to the preservation of their little community's soul and character.

Left: **United States, 1900.**

Various ethnic recipes using corn—such as the Italian polenta made with broth and to which herbs and cheese are often added—have also gained in popularity throughout America.

Contemporary Bread

While corn bread is a traditional favorite, wheat breads now line bakery shelves everywhere. These breads take infinite shapes—round and long loaves, rolls, and breadsticks—and come in a multitude of varieties, such as pumpernickel, rye, sundried tomato, and cinnamon raisin. One American favorite is San Francisco's famous sourdough bread,

Below: **Hot dog.**

a fine wheat flour bread made with leaven. Sourdough bread comes in loaves and in a cannonball shape, which sometimes serves as a bowl for soups, such as New England clam chowder.

Cultural and ethnic diversity has played a significant role in the evolution of bread in the United States. Immigrants from around the world have brought, and continue to bring, bread recipes with them. Americans enjoy Mediterranean pitas, bagels—a New York standard, whose numerous flavors rival those of regular bread—as well as Indian naan, Chinese baked or steamed buns filled with barbecued pork, and Italian focaccia baked with olive oil, salt, and rosemary.

Another American favorite of Italian origin is pizza. Pizza has a dough-base whose thickness de-

SANDWICHES

Left: **An automatic sandwich dispenser in the United States.**

pends on where it is made: a New York crust is thin and crispy, whereas a Chicago-style crust is substantially thicker. Anything beyond the basic pizza elements of tomatoes, olive oil, and cheese is left to the imagination of the baker and the customer. Meats such as pepperoni, sausage, and meatballs, as well as vegetables such as mushrooms and peppers are considered standards. More innovative pizza bakers have created unique pizzas with toppings such as spinach, broccoli, ground lamb, pine nuts, and walnuts. Gourmet pizzas have become more popular in recent years, but many still prefer a simple slice.

With so many kinds and styles of bread widely available, it has become increasingly difficult to maintain that the only breads Americans consume are packaged breads from the supermarket. Even

those breads now reflect the growing demand in America for bread of the highest—and healthiest—quality. Loaves made with organic wheat flour, oat bran, and spelt are often favored over plain white bread. Pre-wrapped bread may be convenient, but as bakery lines attest, fresh bread is well worth a detour.

This bread renaissance in the United States (which actually began in the early 1980s) has not gone unnoticed. Since 1994, American teams have participated in the Coupe du Monde de la Boulangerie. The American team that qualified for the competition in 1994 came in sixth. Two years later, Americans won in the category of specialty bread and baguette and, in 1999, the American team triumphed in Paris, winning bread-baking's world cup over twelve other participating countries.

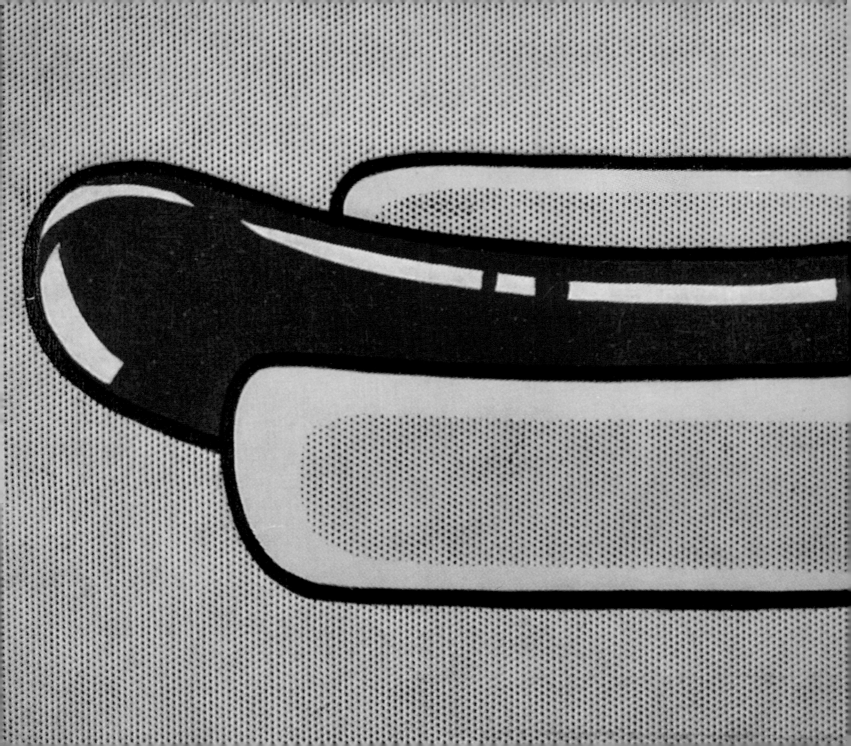

Sandwiches & Co.

It is said that because he did not want to interrupt his card game, John Montague, Fourth Earl of Sandwich (1718–1792), had his cook serve a piece of cold beef between two slices of bread. Thus, the card game was saved, and the sandwich was born.

Since then, the basic idea has evolved, with everyone trying to adapt the bread to fit his or her own personal conception of the sandwich. The gourmets, the lazy, the impatient, have vied with one another in their attempts to slice, stuff, butter, spread, smear, lay out, prepare, garnish, insert, pile up, superimpose or fold every imaginable kind of bread. Quite successfully, at times. In 1900, for instance, someone thought of inserting a hot sausage into an elongated roll and smearing it with mustard: thus was created the popular hot dog, so called for its visual similarity to the sausage-like dachshund. The same year, the first Monte Cristo was served in a café on the Boulevard des Capucines in Paris: two slices of sandwich bread, Gruyère cheese, and lean ham, a basic combination. The hamburger's origins are somewhat more obscure: this Hamburg Steak is supposed to have been introduced in the United States by German immigrants in the 1880s. The reference to Hamburg has been lost, the steak has remained, chopped, served on a round roll, on a bed of lettuce, topped with a tomato slice, various sauces, and sometimes with melted cheese.

Pita, *pan-bagnat, panini,* Tunisian sandwich, bruschetta, pizza—there are a thousand-and-one ways in today's world. Bread has become a serving plate, like the *tranchoirs* of the Middle Ages, those thin slices of whole grain bread upon which the slicing squire laid pieces of boiled or roasted meat. One wonders what Lord Montague would have thought.

BREADS OF ASIA

Japan Enters the *Pan* Era

In the country of rice, bread (or *pan*) has made a substantial impact in the marketplace. The Japanese eat 30 kg of it a year, half of the current French consumption.

Bread was actually introduced into Japan by the Portuguese in the sixteenth century, but only began to succeed commercially with the arrival of the Americans after 1945, when American flour and sandwich bread relieved the wartime shortages. The Japanese adapted to these new tastes and textures, creating a bean-paste filling for bread and for local pastries shaped in decorative wooden molds. The well-known Raymond Calvel, a professor at the French Flour Milling School, joined Yukio Fujii, who had opened an industrial bakery in Kobe (Fujii Panya, later called Donq); Donq bakeries are multiplying in Japan, with Philippe Bigot as their advisor.

Other bakery chains are also thriving, with such names as Saint-Germain and Pompadour, and so are stores with a more artisan orientation, such as Monthabor, Allez France, or Le lys d'or. They offer some sixty types of bread: black bread, yeast bread, country loaves, egg bread, and even seaweed bread.

Authentic French bakers have arrived and opened shops, which number about 50 in Japan today, including Vincent Brûlé with his nine "l'Ami du Pain" bakeries, Dominique Doucet, and Pierre Bush. Bernard Ganachaud opened a bakery in Tokyo in 1984, and he now advises 19 stores. Japan has entered the *pan* era.

Chinese Baguettes

A traditional form of steamed bread is prevalent in Northern China and Beijing, and is also distributed widely in Cambodia, Laos, Thailand, and Vietnam. The dough contains wheat flour, salt, a little sugar, shortening, and yeast.

Right: **Itinerant vendors of French-style bread, Vietnam.**

Round balls of it are placed in stacked bamboo baskets enclosed in a covered pot, where the bread rounds cook at a boiling temperature for about twenty minutes. Before being cooked, they may be stuffed with chopped meat (finely ground pork) or with shrimps or vegetables, with the dough forming pockets that are folded, knotted, and wrapped around the filling.

North China also uses various forms of hard wheat that are unsuitable for bread-making. The unleavened dough is rolled out thinly and sliced into strips, which are left to dry. The Italians prepare their hard-wheat pasta using the same technique, which has been credited to Marco Polo.

Thousands of years of tradition were confronted when the first French bakery in China opened in Beijing in 1984; others have followed in the provinces. The Machines Bertrand bread-oven manufacturer from Nevers is operating a facility that delivers frozen dough ready for baking at points of sale. Using the same momentum, he has also opened café-bakeries selling sandwiches and pizzas—all using French bread.

Pages 228–229: **Market flatbread, decorated with wooden bread stamp or hen feather marker. Kachgar, Chinese Turkestan.**

Opposite: **Breakfast bread from a Mauritanian market.**

Below: **Steamed Chinese dumplings in stacked baskets. China.**

BREADS OF AFRICA

In Africa today, bread has become city food: at breakfast time, employees stop at food stands to have their bowl of Nescafe with milk and sugar, and their slices of bread spread with margarine. The traditional millet gruel and roasted peanuts are virtually forgotten as soon as consumer income rises.

The bakeries don't all offer the same quality: most customers prefer the very tender textured breads with a pale crust (sandwich bread), unlike the expatriates whose taste runs to a crisp golden crust.

Imported Flour

All the bread is made from wheat flour imported from Europe. This raw material is costly and deliveries are not always on schedule. As a result, the flour is mixed to a greater or lesser extent with corn or millet meal, resulting in different colors and textures of dough.

In the countryside, on the other hand, bread is not very common. While it may be available at some markets or storefronts, it is not made at home, where the preferred fare is boiled cereal gruel, or tubers boiled in water, pounded, or made into paste.

In English-speaking countries particularly, women sell clusters of bread made of a light, sweet, brioche-like dough. These rolls, packed in transparent plastic bags, are stacked in baskets carried on the woman's head and sold at markets, street crossings, bus terminals, and cab stands. They are crunchy and sometimes slightly grainy. Even the French-speaking countries on the Gulf of Guinea are gradually adopting them.

Bread here is a foreign food, an element of access to a more comfortable way of life, and one which is slowly replacing some of the traditional dishes served at mealtime.

SELECTED BREAD RECIPES

As an indispensable complement to any regime of balanced nourishment, bread is present in one form or another at many meals, and is to be found on tables all over the world. Moreover, to knead some rich dough by hand and then bring forth from the oven a pan full of good hot bread provides a savory pleasure that delights gourmands everywhere. From white bread to *fougasse,* from bagels to *tortillas,* we have selected a number of typical recipes from around the world—an unusual but delicious way of traveling to the four corners of the globe.

White Bread

The popular image of France is not complete without a golden, crusty baguette. Let us hope that this national icon, currently undergoing so many taste changes, will be saved through the good offices of a few conscientious bakers. This basic recipe can also be used for other breads in various forms (small rolls, *ficelle, bâtard, marguerite, épi*), as well as pizzas, *tartes flambées,* or any other dish calling for bread dough.

3 baguettes

- 1²/₃ tablespoons active dry yeast
- 1¹/₂ cups lukewarm water
- 2 teaspoons salt
- 4 cups unbleached white flour
- 1 cup whole wheat flour

1. In a large bowl, dissolve yeast in one-third of the water and let it rest for 5 minutes.

2. Dissolve 1 teaspoon of salt in the remaining water.

3. Mix the flours in a large bowl and make a well in the center. Pour in the yeast and water mixture, and work thoroughly until smooth.

4. Turn out the dough on a work surface and knead it, stretching and lifting it for at least 10 minutes; the dough should be smooth, flexible, and elastic.

5. Gather the dough into a ball, return it to the bowl and cover with a cloth (dampen the cloth if the room is hot and dry). Let the dough rise for about 30 minutes or until it doubles in volume (the fermentation time depends on room temperature, ideally about 75 degrees).

6. Punch down the dough, and shape as desired (baguette or rolls). Let it rise on the baking sheet for another 30 minutes.

7. Heat the oven to 400°F. Dissolve the remaining teaspoon of salt in ¹/₂ cup of water and brush the surface of the shaped dough with this mixture. Thoroughly spray the oven's interior with water and insert the baking sheet. Bake for 20 minutes. Repeat the brushing and spraying twice during this time. Lower the oven temperature to 350°F. Continue baking another five minutes. Let the bread cool on a rack.

Whole Grain Country Bread

Since the advent of dietetics and the trend toward organic products, bread made from whole grain flour, which had long been considered coarse and was usually reserved for people of modest means, is now on the verge of displacing white bread. This recipe is based on whole wheat flour, but can be adapted to different grains (barley, rye, oats, spelt), as long as one-half of the mixture is wheat flour to ensure a light, airy texture.

1 large square loaf
- 5 teaspoons active dry yeast
- 2 cups lukewarm water
- 5 cups whole wheat flour
- 1½ teaspoons salt
- 1 tablespoon vegetable oil (or melted butter), plus additional
- 2 tablespoons oats or sunflower seeds for decoration

1. In a large bowl, dissolve the yeast in 1 cup lukewarm water.

2. Combine the flour and salt. Gradually stir into the yeast, along with the remaining water, and oil or butter. Mix thoroughly and work the dough vigorously; it will seem sticky and too wet at first, but the whole wheat flour will gradually absorb the extra moisture as the mixture is kneaded.

3. Set the dough on a work surface and continue kneading for 10 minutes. Roll into a ball, coat with oil, and replace in clean bowl. Cover with a damp cloth and let rest 2 hours at room temperature.

4. Place the dough on a floured work surface, punch it down, and knead it for a few minutes.

5. Shape the dough into 1 large loaf and place in greased pan. Cover with damp cloth and let rise 40 to 60 minutes at room temperature, or until double in volume.

6. Preheat the oven to 350°F. Sprinkle the dough with the oats or sunflower seeds and bake for about 30 to 40 minutes. The bottom of the bread should sound hollow when rapped lightly. Let cool on a rack. This bread is even better the next day.

Olive Bread

The unique flavor of olives gives a Mediterranean accent to this bread, to be savored like cake, unless eaten with fresh goat cheese, Parma ham, or sun-ripened crudités.

1. In a medium-size bowl dissolve the yeast in half the warm water.

2. Mix the salt into the yeast. Blend in a little flour and add the remaining water, along with the olive oil. Work in the rest of the flour and mix thoroughly. Knead the dough for 5 minutes until it is smooth and elastic.

3. Roll the dough into a ball, set it into a greased bowl, and cover with a damp cloth. Let rest 1 hour at room temperature.

4. Punch down the dough on a work surface sprinkled with flour. Roll it into a 10-inch circle. Distribute the olives over one half of the circle and make three deep cuts in the other side using a sharp, pointed knife. Fold the cut side over the olive-covered half. Seal the edges thoroughly, moistening with a little water if necessary.

1 medium-size loaf
- 1¼ tablespoons active dry yeast
- ¾ cup lukewarm water
- ½ teaspoon salt
- 2 cups whole wheat flour
- 2 tablespoons olive oil
- 4 ounces pitted black olives

5. Lightly grease a baking sheet and gently place the loaf on it. Cover with a cloth and let rise for 40 minutes.

6. Preheat the oven to 425°F. Brush the loaf with a little olive oil. Bake for 30 to 40 minutes. Serve warm.

Cheese Bread

Bread dough lends itself to all sorts of plain and fancy garnishes and this cheese bread is a perfect example: Use Emmentaler, as in this recipe, or choose a stronger cheese like Cantal, Parmesan, or Mimolette. This bread is always delicious served as a hot appetizer with cocktails or with a vegetable soup.

1 round loaf
- 2 cups whole wheat flour
- ³/₄ cup lukewarm water
- 1 teaspoon salt
- 1¹/₄ tablespoons active dry yeast
- 8 ounces grated Emmentaler or Swiss cheese

1. In a large bowl, dissolve the yeast in ¹/₂ cup of the water.

2. Gradually blend in the flour, remaining warm water, and salt. Knead for 10 minutes until the dough is very smooth. Roll it into a ball and let it rest covered with a damp cloth for 30 to 40 minutes, until it doubles in bulk.

3. Turn out onto a lightly floured board and knead again for 5 minutes. Carefully blend in two-thirds of the grated cheese.

4. Roll out the dough into a 1-inch-thick circle, place on floured baking sheet, and let it rest again 20 minutes at room temperature.

5. Preheat the oven to 425°F. Sprinkle the dough with the remaining cheese, and bake for 15 minutes. Lower the oven temperature if the cheese is browning too quickly. Serve hot.

Polka Bread

This bread is found in many regions, but its exact origin is difficult to establish. It is distinguished by its flattened shape and a thick crust scored into a checkerboard pattern. In former times, children used to tear the bread along this squared design rather than cut it in slices.

1 large loaf
- 2¹/₂ tablespoons active dry yeast
- 1¹/₄ cups water
- 1¹/₂ teaspoons salt (minus one large pinch reserved for glazing)
- 4¹/₂ cups whole wheat flour

1. Prepare the dough according to the first four steps of the recipe for white bread.

2. Roll dough into a ball and place it in the bowl. Cover it tightly with plastic wrap and let it ferment for 24 to 36 hours in the refrigerator.

3. Take the dough out of the refrigerator and let it rest 20 minutes until it reaches room temperature.

4. Roll the dough into a ball and stretch it with the palm of the hand into a 12-inch circle. Place it on a floured baking sheet and let it rest for 20 minutes.

5. Preheat the oven to 400°F. Flatten the dough once more as much as possible to eliminate most of the extra gas resulting from fermentation. Score the surface deeply in a criss-cross pattern, using the blade of a sharp pointed knife.

6. Brush the polka bread with a little saltwater and bake for about 25 to 30 minutes. Lower the temperature if the bread is browning too quickly.

Pretzels

This specialty, originally from Eastern Europe, is named after the Latin *bracellae* meaning "little arms." The early Christians were the first to eat Lenten bread in the shape of a cross with intersecting branches, very similar to today's pretzel. The dough for this recipe is cooked twice: first in boiling water for a tender texture, then in the oven to a golden color, covered with crunchy coarse salt.

16 pretzels

- 1²/₃ tablespoons active dry yeast
- ²/₃ cup, plus 2 tablespoons lukewarm water
- ¹/₂ cup lukewarm milk
- 3¹/₂ cups fine wheat flour
- 1 teaspoon salt
- 2¹/₂ tablespoons melted butter
- 1 egg yolk beaten with a little milk for glazing
- Coarse salt

1. Dissolve yeast in water and milk.

2. Put the flour in a large bowl and add the salt, yeast mixture, and melted butter. Mix the ingredients carefully, then turn out the dough on a work surface and knead for 10 minutes until it is flexible and elastic.

3. Gather up the dough into a ball, place it in the bowl, cover it with a cloth and let it rest for 60 minutes at room temperature.

4. Punch down the dough and knead it again for 5 minutes. Form 16 balls of dough and roll each one into a cylinder 12 inches long, to the thickness of the thumb. Fold each cylinder into a U-shape and bring back the ends to the center, after crossing them in an X-shape. Set them one by one on the floured work surface and cover with a cloth. Let them rest 10 minutes.

5. Meanwhile, boil some salted water in a large saucepan. Lower the heat and plunge the pretzels into the simmering water. As soon as they float to the surface, remove them with a skimmer and blot them gently with a clean cloth.

6. Preheat the oven to 400°F. Set the pretzels on one or more buttered baking sheets. Brush them with the beaten egg and sprinkle them with coarse salt. Bake about 30 minutes until they are golden. Cool on a rack.

Tortillas

These small flatbreads were the basic nourishment of the Aztec and Maya people. Made from ground corn, *tortillas* are used in an infinite number of recipes in Mexican cookery: chicken-filled *tacos*, melted cheese *quesadillas*, *enchiladas* heaped with guacamole or refried beans. Mexicans also enjoy *tortillas* at cocktail time, cut into small triangles and fried in boiling oil to make chips. Since the cornmeal for *tortillas* may sometimes be difficult to obtain, this equally tasty recipe has been adapted for wheat flour.

12 *tortillas*

- 2 cups whole wheat flour
- 1¹/₂ tablespoons baking powder
- 1¹/₂ teaspoons salt
- 4 tablespoons butter or lard
- ²/₃ cup, plus 2 tablespoons hot water

1. Mix the flour, baking powder, and salt in a large bowl or pan. Cut the butter or lard in small pieces and blend it in with as little handling as possible; pour in a little hot water to form a pliable dough that can be rolled into a ball. Let it stand 20 minutes at room temperature.

2. Form 12 small balls and let them rest covered with a cloth.

3. Dust the work surface with flour, and flatten each ball as thinly as possible into a circle with a rolling pin. Keep dusting the work surface with flour as needed.

4. Heat a smooth cast-iron griddle or a nonstick frying pan. Do not grease. Cook the *tortillas* for about 1 minute on one side and turn them over as soon as small bubbles appear on the surface. Continue cooking for 1 or 2 minutes on the second side.

5. Keep the cooked *tortillas* warm in a cloth-covered basket until ready to serve.

Saffron Bread

Saffron, in great demand since the Middle Ages for its powerful aroma and beautiful golden hue, is nothing more than the pollen or pistil of the crocus bloom. At one time, the Cornwall region of England specialized in its cultivation, and housewives quite logically thought of using it to flavor this delicate bread.

1 square loaf
- 2½ tablespoons active dry yeast
- 1 cup lukewarm milk, plus additional
- 1 pinch saffron powder or pistils
- ½ pound butter (1 stick)
- 1 cup sugar
- 4 cups cake flour
- ½ teaspoon salt
- 1 egg yolk
- ⅔ cup coarsely chopped almonds

1. Dissolve the yeast in ½ cup of the milk, and the saffron in 2 tablespoons of boiling water.

2. Melt the butter and sugar in the remaining milk, which should be hot, but not boiling. Let cool to lukewarm.

3. Put the flour and salt in a large bowl and hollow out a well in the center. Put in the dissolved yeast, milk/butter/sugar mixture, saffron, and egg yolk. Mix carefully, first with a spatula, then by hand, until the dough is well blended. Turn it out on a work surface and knead for 5 minutes.

4. Put the dough in a bowl covered with a cloth and let it stand for 1 hour at room temperature.

5. Butter a loaf pan. Punch down the dough by pressing hard with the palm of the hand and mix in the chopped almonds, making sure they are evenly distributed.

6. Pack the dough into the pan, cover with a cloth and let it rise for 40 minutes at room temperature.

7. Preheat the oven to 350°F. Brush the surface of the bread with a little milk and bake for 30 to 40 minutes. Unmold while still warm and finish cooling on a rack.

Fougasse

Fougasse (or *fouace*, or *focaccia* in Italian) was originally a sort of unleavened wheat flatbread cooked under the ashes of the fireplace. In fact, its name comes from the Latin word *focus*, meaning hearth. This basic recipe may be enriched with onions, olives, anchovy filets, or finely diced, grilled salt pork or fatback, as in Provence.

1 large *fougasse*
- ~ 1²/₃ tablespoons active dry yeast
- ~ 1¹/₄ cups lukewarm water
- ~ 6 tablespoons olive oil, plus additional
- ~ 1 teaspoon salt
- ~ 4 cups whole wheat flour

1. In a large bowl, dissolve the yeast in the water. Add 3 tablespoons of oil and the salt. Mix well. Blend in the flour and mix again to make a dough that is smooth but not sticky.

2. Continue kneading the dough on a floured surface for about 10 minutes. Roll the dough into a ball, brush with a little oil, and place it in a large bowl. Cover with a damp cloth and let rise 2 hours at room temperature.

3. Turn out the dough on a floured work surface. Punch it down and flatten it out by hand to shape it into a fairly long oval. Fold the dough twice, forming three layers, crimp edges together with fingers, and let the dough rest again for 10 minutes.

4. Stretch out the dough with a rolling pin into an oval about 12-inches long and ¹/₂-inch thick. Place the shaped dough on a lightly oiled baking sheet and let it rest once more for 1 hour.

5. Preheat the oven to 425°F. With a pointed knife, make eight deep cuts, almost all the way through the dough, from a center line out, to form a lengthwise design like the ridge pattern on a leaf or like kernels along an ear of wheat. Brush the *fougasse* with the remaining olive oil and bake for about 25 minutes. Cool on a rack.

Grissini

These crisp golden breadsticks originated in Turin and are found on every Italian restaurant table in their individual paper wrappings. They make an irresistible, delicious snack while one is waiting to be served. They can be seasoned before baking with herbs like oregano, thyme, and rosemary, or sprinkled with coarse salt or parmesan.

Makes about 2 dozen *grissini*
- ~ 1³/₄ teaspoons active dry yeast
- ~ 1 teaspoon sugar
- ~ 1 cup lukewarm water
- ~ 3³/₄ cups unbleached white flour
- ~ 1 teaspoon salt
- ~ 4 tablespoons olive oil

GLAZE
- ~ 1 egg white
- ~ 1 teaspoon water

- ~ Poppy seeds, sesame seeds, or rosemary, optional

1. In a large bowl, dissolve the yeast and sugar in the water for about 10 minutes.

2. Add the flour, salt, and olive oil. Mix well to obtain a fairly stiff dough with the consistency of pie crust (add a little water if the dough is too thick). Place the dough on a work surface and knead for 10 minutes until smooth, soft, and elastic.

3. Put the kneaded dough in a bowl and let rest, covered, for about 1 hour at room temperature.

4. Preheat oven to 425°F. Punch down the dough and stretch it out with a rolling pin into a rectangle about ¹/₄-inch thick.

5. Cut the dough into strips with a knife and roll them lightly between your fingers into cylinders about 10- to 12-inches long.

6. Place the *grissini* on lightly oiled or floured baking sheet. Combine the egg white and water. Brush the *grissini* with the glaze and sprinkle them with any seeds of your choice.

7. Bake for 10 to 15 minutes, turning the *grissini* halfway through the baking so that they acquire a golden color all over. The baking time depends on one's preference for light or dark color.

Bagels

These rolls with a hole in the middle, originally Jewish and now beloved of all New Yorkers, were brought to the United States by Polish immigrants at the beginning of the century. American bakers let their imagination run wild to invent variations on this theme: poppy seeds, caraway, sesame, onions, or cinnamon and raisins—the choices are infinite. As a result, people can indulge in bagels all day long, dipped in their breakfast coffee or as sandwiches with cream cheese and smoked salmon.

12 bagels

- 2½ teaspoons active dry yeast
- 1 teaspoon sugar
- ⅓ cup water
- ⅓ cup milk
- 1 large egg
- 2 tablespoons butter, melted, or oil
- 2½ cups unbleached white flour
- 1 teaspoon salt
- Poppy or sesame seeds, caraway, coarse salt, or cinnamon, optional

1. Put the yeast and sugar in a medium-size bowl. Combine the milk and water and pour over them. Let stand to dissolve.

2. Separate the egg and beat the white lightly, reserving yolk. Add to the yeast mixture along with the melted butter (or oil). Stir in the flour and salt and blend them to obtain a soft, homogenous dough. Turn out onto a lightly floured board and knead for 10 minutes, until the dough becomes smooth and elastic.

3. Place the dough in a greased bowl and cover with a damp cloth. Let rise until double in bulk.

4. Punch down the dough by flattening it with the palm of the hand. Divide it into 12 pieces and shape them into small balls. Flatten them slightly and push your index finger through the middle to make a hole. Widen the opening as much as possible by stretching the dough between the thumb and index finger, as it will shrink during the second rising. Shape and plump the bagels to make them uniform in appearance.

5. Cover the bagels with a cloth and let them rise at room temperature for about 20 minutes.

6. Preheat the oven to 400°F. Meanwhile, bring about 3 quarts of water to a boil in a large pot. Add the bagels, three or four at a time, into the gently boiling water. Cook for 3 minutes, turn, and cook about another 3 minutes. Remove with a slotted spoon and drain them on a cloth. Set on a lightly greased baking sheet about one inch apart.

7. Brush the bagels with the egg yolk beaten with a little water, and sprinkle with seeds, salt, or other garnish if desired. Bake in the oven for about 20 minutes until they are golden.

Austrian Kugelhopf

This type of buttery egg bread is found throughout Eastern Europe, from Austria to Alsace (where a salty version is made with walnuts and diced bacon.) This is a traditional festive cake that plays a highly symbolic role at many weddings, when the groom's family offers the new daughter-in-law a decorated earthenware mold along with the family recipe.

1 large kugelhopf
- ~ 1²/₃ tablespoons active dry yeast
- ~ ²/₃ cup plus 2 tablespoons lukewarm milk
- ~ ¹/₃ cup granulated sugar
- ~ 3 cups whole wheat flour
- ~ ¹/₂ teaspoon salt
- ~ 3 large eggs
- ~ ¹/₂ pound (2 sticks) butter, softened
- ~ ³/₄ cup raisins
- ~ About 20 shelled whole almonds
- ~ Confectioner's sugar for glazing

1. Dissolve the yeast in the milk. Add the sugar and mix.

2. Mix the flour and salt in a large bowl. Hollow out the center and add the yeast mixture. Blend in a little flour and as soon as the dough begins to offer some resistance, add one egg. Continue blending in all the flour and eggs.

3. Mix thoroughly by hand for 5 minutes, then gradually add in the butter. Continue working the mixture until the dough is absolutely smooth, very elastic and glossy. It should pull away from the sides of the bowl.

4. Cover the bowl with a damp cloth and let rest for 60 minutes.

5. Meanwhile, soak the raisins in a little hot water or tea. Generously butter a kugelhopf mold and decorate each scalloped section around the central tube with whole almonds. Set aside in refrigerator.

6. Drain the raisins. Punch down the dough, which should have doubled in volume, pressing on it thoroughly to release all the fermentation gases. Blend in the raisins.

7. Pack the dough into the mold and cover once again with a damp cloth. Let it stand for 40 minutes until the dough has risen nearly to the top of the mold.

8. Preheat the oven to 350°F. Bake the kugelhopf for 30 to 40 minutes, taking care not to let the top get too brown.

9. Cool before unmolding on a rack. Dust with confectioner's sugar before serving.

Swiss Braided Bread

In Switzerland, this attractive bread is prominently displayed at the Sunday breakfast table. It is served with butter, honey, and jam, but since it contains no sugar, it is also eaten with cheese or cold cuts and makes very fine sandwiches. It should not be left to rise too long or at too warm a temperature to ensure that it will keep its shape during baking.

1 large or 2 medium braids
- ⅔ cup milk
- ⅔ cup creme fraîche
- 2⅔ tablespoons active dry yeast
- 4½ cups unbleached flour
- 2 teaspoons salt
- 4 tablespoons (½ stick) butter, at room temperature
- 1 large egg, beaten
- 1 egg yolk beaten with a little milk for glazing

1. Over a low flame, heat the milk and creme fraîche until lukewarm. Remove from the heat, and dissolve the yeast in the milk mixture.

2. Put the flour in a large bowl and hollow out a well in the center for the yeast mixture and salt. Combine with your fingertips and gradually blend in the softened butter and the beaten egg.

3. Take the dough out of the bowl and knead it on a floured work surface for about 10 minutes. When it is elastic and smooth, put the dough in a lightly buttered bowl. Cover with plastic wrap or a damp towel and let rest at room temperature for about 1 hour; the dough should double in volume.

4. Punch down the dough and roll it into a ball. Divide it into three pieces, and roll each into a cylinder 10-inches long.

5. Join the three cylinders together at one end, brushing with a little glaze, if necessary, to bind them. Braid the dough and close by firmly pressing the ends together.

6. Carefully place the braid on a baking sheet and let rest for about 20 minutes, or until it rises slightly.

7. Preheat the oven to 400°F. Brush the braided loaf with the egg yolk glaze, being careful not to let the glaze drip onto the baking sheet. Bake for about 40 minutes. Serve lukewarm.

Viennese Baguette

The venerable Austrian capital has earned fame in the annals of pastry artistry through its mastery of leavened and flaky doughs, fashioned into delicious specialty breads, rolls, and danish. This fame has unfortunately made us forget that it was these same Viennese bakers who perfected the beloved baguette! Today's Viennese baguette is a deluxe variation, easily identified by its twisted form, its tender texture, and its faintly sweet flavor.

2 baguettes or 8 rolls
- 1⅔ tablespoons active dry yeast
- 1¼ cups lukewarm water
- 4 cups whole wheat flour
- 1 teaspoon salt
- 1 tablespoon sugar
- 1⅔ tablespoons powdered milk
- 1 tablespoon butter, softened
- A little milk for glazing

1. Dissolve yeast in a little of the water.

2. Mix the flour, salt, sugar, and powdered milk in a large bowl. Hollow out a well in the center for the yeast. Mix carefully, gradually adding the remaining water. When the dough is flexible, blend in the butter and knead for 10 minutes on a work surface.

3. Roll the dough into a ball and let it stand in the bowl for 3 hours, covered with a damp towel. Punch down the dough vigorously every hour.

4. Punch down the dough one last time and break it in two. Shape each piece into a long baguette and set side by side on a floured baking sheet. Let them rest about 60 minutes.

5. Preheat the oven to 425°F. Cut slashes 1 inch apart along the top of each baguette, using a sharp, pointed knife. Brush with a little fresh milk and bake for 20 to 25 minutes.

Gingerbread

Gingerbread is said to have come to the attention of **Philippe le Bon** in Flanders, where he took such a liking to this "bee syrup cake" that he brought the recipe back to Dijon. This specialty, which is really a cake requiring neither kneading nor leavening, is in fact found throughout Northern Europe. Each region has its own recipe and traditional shape derived from popular legend or custom, such as the German Saint Nicholas or the little New Year piglet.

1 large gingerbread
- 7 ounces honey
- 1 cup sugar
- ²/₃ cup plus 2 tablespoons milk
- ¹/₄ pound butter (1 stick)
- ¹/₂ teaspoon ground anise
- ¹/₂ teaspoon ground ginger
- ¹/₂ teaspoon ground cinnamon
- Pinch of grated nutmeg
- Pinch of ground clove
- Grated peel of 1 lemon
- 1¹/₂ cups whole wheat flour
- 1¹/₂ cups rye flour
- 2¹/₂ teaspoons active dry yeast
- 3¹/₂ ounces candied citrus peel or ginger
- 1 tablespoon shredded almonds, optional

1. Melt the honey, sugar, milk, and butter together over low heat. Add the ground spices and grated lemon peel.

2. Add this mixture to the rye and wheat flour blended with the yeast. Mix thoroughly to obtain a homogeneous dough. Blend in the candied fruit.

3. Preheat the oven to 320°F. Butter a loaf pan and sprinkle the bottom with shredded almonds. Fill it with the cake dough and bake for about 40 minutes. A knife blade inserted into the cake should come out dry.

4. Cool to lukewarm temperature and unmold on a rack. The gingerbread is best if stored for 48 hours before eating.

Walnut Raisin Bread

This bread, rustic and refined at the same time, combines some particularly compatible flavors: the sweetness of raisins, the nutty taste of walnuts, and the slight tang of rye flour. The bread is especially good with fresh or ripened cheeses, but it is also delicious toasted at breakfast with butter and honey.

1 large square or round loaf
- $1^1/_2$ cups mixed milk and water
- $2^2/_3$ tablespoons active dry yeast
- $2^1/_2$ cups whole wheat flour, approximately
- 3 cups rye flour
- $1^1/_2$ teaspoons salt
- 1 cup walnuts, chopped
- $^1/_2$ cup raisins

1. Heat the water and milk mixture to lukewarm temperature and dissolve the yeast in $^1/_2$ cup of the warm liquid.

2. Mix both flours and salt in a large bowl. Make a well in the center for the yeast mixture and the remaining water and milk. Add and mix until the dough is soft but not sticky.

3. Turn out the dough on a floured work surface and knead for 10 minutes, until nicely firm and elastic. Place it in a bowl covered with a damp cloth and let it stand for 3 hours at room temperature.

4. Turn out the dough on a work surface and punch it down. Roll it out and spread out the nuts and raisins on its surface. Fold over and press down several times so that the filling is evenly distributed.

5. Shape the dough into a ball or pack it into a lightly oiled loaf pan. Cover with a cloth and let it rise for about $1^1/_2$ hours.

6. Preheat the oven to 350°F. Brush the surface with a little water and bake for about 45 minutes. Unmold the loaf and cool on a rack. This bread is even better the next day.

Pita Bread

This type of fine flatbread is very popular throughout the Middle East. It is baked in a traditional oven where it quickly puffs out very dramatically. It collapses just as fast but still forms a sort of pocket which can be stuffed with grilled meat, raw vegetables, or falafel.

8 pitas
- 1 tablespoon active dry yeast
- 1 cup lukewarm water
- 2 cups unbleached white flour
- 1 cup whole wheat flour
- 1 teaspoon salt
- 1 tablespoon olive oil, plus additional

1. In a large bowl, dissolve the yeast in the water. Add the flours and salt, and mix vigorously. Work the dough for 5 minutes and add the olive oil. Continue for another 5 minutes; turn out the dough on a work surface and knead it with a stretching motion until it becomes pliable and elastic.

2. Rub the dough with oil and place it in a bowl covered with a cloth, and let it stand for 1 to 2 hours, or until doubled in volume.

3. Divide the dough into eight pieces and roll them into balls about the size of a golf ball. Flatten them into $^1/_4$-inch-thick circles, working carefully as you stretch and shape the dough.

4. As you form each pita, set it on a floured work surface and cover. After about 10 minutes, flatten them with a rolling pin.

5. Let the pitas rise once more, for 20 minutes.

6. Lightly oil several baking sheets (or plan to cook the pitas in several batches). Preheat the sheets in a 450°F oven.

7. Set the pitas on the sheets and sprinkle them quickly with a little water. Bake for 4 to 5 minutes, making sure that they do not begin to brown. Check that they are firm and cooked through.

8. Place the pitas on a rack and let them cool briefly. Wrap them carefully in a cloth so they will remain soft.

Notes

1. H. E. Jacob, *Histoire du pain depuis 6,000 ans*, Paris, Le Seuil, 1958, pp. 168–173.

2. J. Montandon, *Le Livre du pain*, Lausanne, Édita, 1974, p. 24.

3. Jacques Barrau, *Le Pain*, Paris, La Courtille, 1979, pp. 13–16.

4. Arminius Vambery, *Voyage d'un faux derviche dans l'Asie centrale*, Paris, Hachette, 1865, p. 76.

5. A. Goursaud, *La Société rurale traditionnelle en Limousin*, Paris, G. P. Maisonneuve, 1976, p. 105.

6. R. J. Bernard, "L'alimentation paysanne en Gévaudan au XVIIIᵉ siecle," in *Annales ESC*, 24, 6, November–December 1969, pp. 1454–1455.

7. Monette Ribeyrol, "Une collecte de pains rituels en Bulgarie," in *Objects et Mondes*, X, 1, Spring 1970, p. 42.

8. Irène Melikoff, "Notes sur les coutumes des Alevis. À propos de quelques fêtes d'Anatolie centrale," in *Quand le crible était dans la paille*, Hommage à P. N. Boratav, G. P. Maisonneuve, 1978, p. 276.

9. Sarah Dars, *Mongolie*, Paris, Le Seuil, Petite Planète, 1979, p. 52.

10. J. Gutwirth, "Les pains azymes de la Pâque chez les *hassidim*," in *Objets et Mondes*, XVI, 4, Winter 1976, p. 148.

11. H. E. Jacob, *op. cit.*, p. 382.

12. A. A. Gura, O. A. Ternovskaja, N. I. Tolstoï, "Les noces de la terre et des hommes," in *Le Courrier de l'Unesco*, août 1978, p. 15.

13. A. Desquant, *Boire et manger en Sancerrois au temps de la cuisine à l'âtre*, Bourges, Desquand, 1977, p. 501.

14. *Rites de la mort*, Musée de l'Homme, 1979, p. 17: Lucienne Roubin, Les Hommes et la mort, Le Sycomore, 1979, p. 47.

15. Jean-Yves Loude, *Rituels funéraires chez les Kalash de l'Hindu-Kush*.

16. Iouri Knorozov, "La vie et au-delà chez les anciens Mayas," in *Le Courrier de l'Unesco*, February 1979, p. 15.

Bibliography

◆ Apfelbaum, M., and R. Lepoutre. *Les Mangeurs inégaux*. Paris: Stock, 1978.

◆ Aron, J.-P. *Le Mangeur du XIXᵉ siècle*. Paris: R. Laffont, 1973.

◆ Arpin, M. *Historique de la meunerie et de la boulangerie depuis les temps préhistoriques jusqu'à l'année 1914*. Paris: Le Chancelier, 1948.

◆ Assire, J. *Le Livre du pain*. Paris: Flammarion, 1996.

◆ Basini, G. L. *L'uomo e il pane. Risorse, consumi e carenze alimentari della popolazione modernese nel cinque e seicento*. Milan, 1970.

◆ Blumel, F., and W. Boog. *500 Jahre Backofen*. Ulm-Donau. Deutsches Brotmuseum, 1977.

◆ Bois, D. *Les Plantes alimentaires chez tous les peuples et à travers les âges. Histoire, utilisation, culture*. Paris: Lechevalier, 1927–1937, 4 vols.

◆ Braudel, F. *Civilisation matérielle, économie et capitalisme, XVᵉ–XVIIIᵉ siècle*. Paris: Armand Colin, 1980.

◆ Breugnot, P., and D. Chegaray. *Boulangeries de Paris*. Paris: Chêne-TF 1, 1978.

◆ Brown, E. E. *The Tassajara Bread Book*. Berkeley: Shambhala Pub., 1970.

◆ Bruneton-Governatori, A. *Le Pain de bois: ethnohistoire de la châtaigne et du châtaignier*. Toulouse: Eché, 1984.

◆ Calvel, R. *La Boulangerie moderne*. Paris: Eyrolles, 1952.

◆ Campbell, A. *Det Svenska Brodet*. Stockholm, 1951.

◆ Carles, E. *Une soupe aux herbes sauvages*. Paris: J.-Cl. Simoen, 1977.

◆ Caufriez, A. *Le Chant du pain. Tràs-os-montes*. Lisbon: Calouste Gulbenkian Foundation, 1997.

◆ Célos, G. *Le Pain brié*. Paris: Éd. Jouve, 1910.

◆ Chatelet, N. *Le Corps à corps culinaire*. Paris: Le Seuil, 1977.

◆ Collister, L., and A. Blake. *Le Grand Livre du pain*. Paris: Grund, 1994.

◆ *Descriptions des Arts et Métiers, faites ou approuvées par M.M. de l'Académie royale des Sciences*. Paris, 1761–1788.

◆ Diderot, and d'Alembert. *L'Encyclopédie, ou Dictionnaire raisonné des Sciences, des Arts et des Métiers*. Paris, 1768.

◆ Dimbleby, G. W., and P. J. Ucko. *The Domestication and Exploitation of Plants and Animals*. London: Duckworth, 1969.

◆ Dupont, J.-C. *Le Pain d'habitant*. Ottawa: Leméac, 1974.

◆ Durand, P., and M. Sarrau. *Le Livre du pain*, Monaco. Éditions du Rocher, 1973.

◆ Encyclopedia Roret. *Meunier*. Paris: L. Mulo. 1910. 2 vols.

◆ Eno, D. *The Little Brown Bread Book*. Winchester, Hants.: Juniper Press, 1976.

◆ Fawzeya-e-Kamal, R. *La Préparation du pain dans un village du delta égyptien, province de Sharqia*. Cairo: Institut français d'archéologie orientale, 1978.

◆ Fenton, C. L., and H. B. Kitchen. *Plants that Feed Us. The Story of Grains and Vegetables*. London: D. Dobson, 1962.

◆ Flandrin, J.-L., and M. Montanari (under the direction of). *Histoire de l'alimentation*. Paris: Fayard, 1996.

◆ Forbes, R. J. *Food and Drink,* in *History of Technology*. Oxford: Clarendon Press, 1954.

◆ Hansen, H. J. *Kunstgeschichte des Backwerks*. Oldenburg: G. Stalling V., 1968.

◆ Hasalová, V. and J. Vajdis. "Trésor de la Tchécoslovaquie." *L'Art populaire*. Paris: Cercle d'art, 1974.

◆ Hieatt, C. B., and Sh. Butler. *Pain, vin et venaison: un livre de cuisine médiévale*. Montreal: Éditions Aurore, 1977.

◆ Jacob, H. E. *Histoire du pain depuis 6,000 ans*. Paris: Le Seuil, 1958.

◆ Kaplan, S. *Le Meilleur Pain du monde*. Paris: Fayard, 1996.

◆ Laffal, F. *Breads of Many Lands*. Essex, Conn.: Gallery Press, 1975.

◆ Lauret, J. C. *Les Fêtes à travers la France*. Paris: Balland, 1972.

◆ Lelong, M. *Le Pain, le Vin et le Fromage*. Forcalquier: Robert Morel, 1972.

◆ Lentéric, B. *Les Maîtres du pain*. Paris: Plon, 1993.

◆ Lombardi, L. *Il Forno e la falce. Eros et Thanathos nella cultura del Pane*. University of Rome: L'Uomo, 1990.

◆ Luraschi, A. *Il Pane e la sua storia*. Turin: L'Arte Bianca, 1953.

◆ Macherel, C. *Une vie de pain. Faire, penser et dire le pain en Europe*. Brussels: Crédit communal, 1994.

◆ Maget, M. *Le Pain anniversaire*. Paris: Éditions. Archives contemporaines, 1989.

◆ *Man and his Foods: Studies in the Ethno-botany of Nutrition, Contemporary, Primitive, and Prehistoric Non-European Diets*. Alabama: The Univ. of Alabama Press, 1973.

◆ Maurizio, A. *Histoire de l'alimentation depuis la préhistoire jusqu'à nos jours*. Paris: Payot, 1932.

◆ Meiv, E. A. *Das susse Basel (Backmodel, Rezepte, Abbildungen)*. Basel: Birkhauser, 1973.

◆ Mercier, L.-S. *Tableau de Paris*. Paris, 1781. Reprint. Geneva: Slatkine, 1970.

◆ Molina, B. J. *The Palestinian Manna Tradition. The Manna Tradition in the Palestinian Targums and its Relationship to the New Testament Writings*. Leiden: Brill, 1968.

◆ Montandon, J. *Le Livre du pain*. Lausanne: Edita, 1974.

◆ Morel, A. *Histoire illustrée de la boulangerie en France*. Paris: Syndicat patronal de la boulangerie de Paris et de la Seine, 1924.

◆ Parmentier M. *Le Parfait Boulanger*. Paris: Imprimerie Royale, 1778.

◆ Poilâne, L. *Faire son pain soi-même*. Paris: Dessain and Tolra, 1982.

◆ ———. *Guide de l'amateur de pain*. Paris: R. Laffont, 1981.

◆ Pomeranz, Y. *Bread Science and Technology*. Westport, Conn.: The Avi Pub. Co., 1971.

◆ *Pour une histoire de l'alimentation*. Collection of works presented by J. J. Hemardinguer. Cahier des Annales 28. Paris: A. Colin, 1970.

◆ Pyke, M. *L'Homme et ses aliments*. Paris: Hachette, 1970.

◆ Rivals, C. *Le Moulin à vent et le meunier*. Paris: Serg/Berger-Levrault, 1988.

◆ Sebillot, P. *Traditions et superstitions de la boulangerie*. Paris, 1891.

◆ Serand, L. *Le Pain, Fabrication rationnelle, historique*. Paris, 1911.

◆ Smith, R. E. F., and David Christian. *Bread and Salt: A Social History and Economic History of Food and Drink in Russia*. Cambridge: University Press, 1984.

◆ Stanway, Dr. A. *Mangez le brut pour bien manger*. Paris: Tchou, 1977.

◆ Tardieu, S. *Equipement et activités domestiques (le pain, la pâtisserie)*. ethnological guides 10/11. Paris: Musée des Arts et Traditions populaires, 1972.

◆ Teti, V. *Il pane, la beffa e la festa: cultural alimentare e ideologia dell'alimentazione nelle classi subalterne*. Rimini: Guaraldi, 2nd ed., 1978.

◆ Texier, E. *Le Tableau de Paris*. Paris. 1852. 2 vols. 1,500 engravings.

◆ Thouvenot, C. *Le Pain d'autrefois. Chroniques alimentaires d'un monde qui s'en va*. Paris: A. Leson, 1976.

◆ Toschi, P. *Arte populare italiana*. Rome: C. Bestelli, 1960.

◆ Toussaint-Samat, M. *Histoire naturelle et morale de la nourriture*. Paris: Bordas, 1987.

◆ Tremolières, J., *La Nutrition*. Paris: Dunod, 1977.

◆ Van Gennep, A. *Manuel de folklore français contemporain*. Paris: Picard, 1937–1958.

◆ Veyne, P. *Le Pain et le Cirque*. Paris: Le Seuil, 1977.

◆ Vielfaure, N., and A. C. Beauviala. *Fêtes, coutumes et gâteaux*. Le Puy. Ch. Bonneton, éd. 1978.

◆ Weiner, P. *Formes à pains d'épices en bois sculpté*. Budapest: Corvina, 1964.

◆ White, J. *The Art of Breadmaking*. London, 1828.

◆ Zaborowski, S. *Le Blé en Asie et en Europe et le culte du pain*. Paris: Alcan, 1906.

◆ Ziehr, W. *Le pain, paysan, meunier, boulanger*. Tielt, Belgium: Éditions Lannoo, 1984.

List of Illustrations

Index

Note: Page numbers in **boldface** refer to recipes.

Photo Credits

AMIENS, Musée de Picardie: 28–29 – ANVERS, Koninklijk Museum voor Schone Kunsten: 154–155 – COURBEVOIE, Photothèque culinaire: 6, 173, 186 g, 212, 213, 217, 245 – PARIS, ■ AKG Photo: 13, 15, 16–17, 19, 22, 26, 30–31, 39, 115, 123, 126–127, 129, 166–167; Cameraphoto: 33; W. Forman: 7, 14; G. Mermet: 23 ■ Archives photographiques de la Médiathèque du Patrimoine/Ministère de la Culture: 50 ■ Artephot/G. Mangin: 52–53; A. Held: 27 ■ Collection Christophe L.: 171 ■ Collection Cinestar: 85 ■ Ciric/B. Cavanagh: 169; A. Pinoges: 231 ■ Dagli Orti: 21, 34 ■ D.R.: 176–177, 182, 224–225 ■ Diaf/J. D. Sudres: 184–185 ■ Diaphor/B. Bonnel: 149 ■ Editing/J.-F. Marin: 94 ■ Fotogram-Stone Images/Hulton Getty: 141, 150; M. Mouchy: 175 ■ Gamma/Bakalian: 66 ■ Marc Garanger: 61 ■ Giraudon: 43, 70, 80–81, 92–93, 114, 148, 151, 195 ■ Hémisphères/P. Frilet: 118 ■ Hoa-Qui/W. Buss: 112–113; B. Debold: 222; M. Huet: 60; J.-D. Joubert: 95; M. Renaudeau: 201; P. Saharoff: 83; N. Thibaut: 110; Valentin: 186 b, 236, 241 ■ Keystone: 51, 56 ■ Jean-Dominique Lajoux: 59 ■ Madame Figaro/J. Caillaut: 158, 163, 187 g ■ Jean Marquis: 116–117, 144 ■ Musée de l'Homme/B. Dupaigne: 74–75, 121, 124–125, 128, 130–131, 132, 133, 134–135, 136, 139, 142–143, 145, 146–147, 157, 183, 192, 198, 210, 211, 214, 219; J. Oster: 10 ■ Nicolas Nilsson: 96–97, 102, 208–209 ■ Option photo/J. Belondrade: 180–181; H. Lenain: 88 ■ Rapho/Network/B. Lewis: 152–153; R. Doisneau: 193; G. Marry: 206; R. & S. Michaud: 68, 69, 73, 78, 79, 98, 99, 108–109, 111; J. Niepce: 159; K. Poulsen: 64–65; H. Silvester: 58, 72, 103, 119, 137, 138 ■ Bernard Richard: 71 ■ RMN/R.G. Ojeda: 44–45 ■ Roger-Viollet: 62, 63, 84, 160–161, 162, 164–165, 179 ■ Selva: 200; Collection Kharbine-Tapabor: 41, 90, 91, 122, 178, 190–191, 215 b ■ Sipa/Corbis/Bettmann: 220, 221 ■ The Image Bank/A. Becker: 205; Petrified collection: 104–105, 196 ■ Top/P. Hussenot: 234–235, 239; G. Mattei/Envision: 186 c, 242–243; Sarramon: 233 ■ Jean Vigne: 37, 40, 215 h – ULM, Brotmuseum: 76–77, 188 – VANVES, Explorer/M. Carbonare: 12; Collection E.S.: 18; J.L.S. Dubois: 100–101; FPG International: 222–223; Geopress: 11; F. Jalain: 199; Mary Evans Picture Library: 36, 49, 54, 55, 57, M. Monck: 218; R. Mattes: 202–203, 226–227, 228–229; J.-P. Nacivet: 8–9; G. Namur: 24–25, 46; Rapa: 230; Schuster/Kiene: 82; A. Tovi: 86–87 ■ Visa/Ginet Drin: 89, 120, 186 h, 187 d, 187 b, 197, 204, 207, 232, 246; A. Lorgnier: 67; F. Zecchin: 107. © ADAGP 1999 for the works of Balthus, Roy Lichtenstein, and Diego Rivera.

Acknowledgments

The author would like to thank the following individuals
for their editing of certain texts:
Jacques Barreau: page 13; Georges Soustelle: "The Tortilla: Bread of Mexico," page 114,
and "Mexico's Bread of the Dead," page 150; Monique de Fontanès: "Ex-votos and the
Pilgrimages of Calabria," page 210; Josette Rivallain: "The Breads of Africa," page 230.

The publishers would like to thank the organization
Espace Pain Information (Paris)
for the documentation it made available.